The Turkish Long-Necked Lute Saz or Bağlama

The Turkish Long-Necked Lute
Saz or Bağlama

Hans de Zeeuw

ARCHAEOPRESS PUBLISHING LTD
Summertown Pavilion
18-24 Middle Way
Summertown
Oxford OX2 7LG
www.archaeopress.com

ISBN 978-1-78969-432-1
ISBN 978-1-78969-433-8 (e-Pdf)

Cover image: Poet-musician playing a tanbûr. Excavated tile ensemble from the summer palace of Sultan Alâ al-Dîn Kayqubâd I, Anatolia, early 13th century. Museum für Islamische Kunst, Staatliche Museen, Berlin. Inv. nr. 00026603.

Bağlama:
'Representing all that is Turkish in music
and all that is musical in the Turk...'
Martin Stokes, *The Arabesk Debate*

for *Hülya*

Contents

Preface and Acknowledgements

Ten years after the Dutch edition of this book, *De Turkse Langhalsluit of Bağlama* (*The Turkish Long-Necked Lute or Bağlama*) it's time for a revised and updated and to a wider audience accessible English edition, the more as publications by authors such as Okan Murat Öztürk, Erol Parlak, Nevzat Çiftçi, and Cihangir Terzi appeared in the meantime. Moreover, new *bağlama* types such as the various *Oğur sazı* types as well as innovative playing techniques and repertory evolved.

The monumental *Folk Musical Instruments of Turkey* (1975) of Laurence Picken is still an important source of information about Turkish folk musical instruments, among which the various Turkish long-necked lutes, containing a wealth of information about their historical background, construction, acoustics, tunings, playing techniques, and terminology.[1] Important Turkish sources are *Ülkelerde Kopuz ve Tezeneli Sazlarımız* (1975) by Mahmut Ragıp Gazimihâl and *Türkiye'de el ile (şelpe) bağlama çalma geleneği ve çalış teknikleri* (2000) by Erol Parlak as well as various articles by authors such as Okan Murat Öztürk, Cihangir Terzi, and Nevzat Çiftçi.[2]

The main focus of this book is the cultural-historical background of the *saz/bağlama*. In additional chapters, the construction, tuning, and playing technique are briefly discussed. The book concludes with a *Glossary of Musical Instruments*, *Discography*, *Bibliography*, *Illustration Credits*, *A Note on Turkish*, and an *Index*. This book is not only intended to be a provisional revision of the official Turkish political-ideological approach of the folk musical traditions of Turkey and the *saz/bağlama*, but also aims initiating further scientific research.

This study benefited from the work of many scholars in various scientific disciplines. It is impossible to credit them all. My intellectual debts are evident from the footnotes and *Bibliography*.

I particularly want to acknowledge the work of Henry George Farmer, Laurence Picken, Jean During, Richard Campbell, Fivos Anoyanakis, Tamila Djani-Zade, Walter Feldman, Ameneh Youssefzadeh, Ricardo Eichmann, Okan Murat Öztürk, and Erol Parlak. For the broader background of my study I have benefited from the work of numerous historians, such as Marshall Hodgson, Jerry Bentley, Joan Aruz, Robert Canfield, Christopher Beckwith, and the late Halil Inalcık, and art historians, such as Stuart Cary Welch, Milo C. Beach, Walter Denny, Norah Titley, Michael Barry, Banu Mahir, and Filiz Cağman.

Many people contributed to this study.

In Turkey, I thank Hüseyin Fırtına and Süleyman Fırtına (Fırtına Müzik Evi, Şirinevler, Istanbul) for introducing me to the construction methods of the *bağlama*. Kemal Eroğlu (Kopuz Saz Evi, Istanbul) for answering my questions about the construction of the *bağlama* and *Oğur sazı*. Okan Murat Öztürk for sharing his knowledge of Turkish folk music and the *bağlama*. Erdal Erzincan for answering my questions about the *şelpe* playing technique and Erkan Oğur for introducing me to the design of the *Oğur sazı*. My gratitude goes to the late Cafer Açın (Enstruman Yapım

---

[1] Picken, L. Folk Musical Instruments of Turkey.
[2] Parlak, E. Türkiye'de el ile (şelpe) bağlama çalma geleneği ve çalış teknikleri.

Bölümü Başkanı, Türk Musikisi Devlet Konservatuarı, Istanbul Teknik Üniversitesi) for his hospitality and introduction to his work as well as his generous permission to use images from his book *Bağlama. Yapım sanatı ve sanatçıları*. The luthier Süleyman Aslan (Dutar Müzik, Istanbul), whom I met in May 2006 at the *Uluslararası Müzik Kongresi* (International Music Gongress) in Istanbul, for sharing his opinion about the traditional construction which according to him no longer meet the requirements made on the contemporary *bağlama*. The luthier Engin Topuzkanamış (Izmir) for generously sharing with me his knowledge about the construction of the *bağlama* and the *Oğur sazı* as well as the various digital images of the construction process of *Oğur sazıs* made by him.

I thank Dr Gülay Yurdal-Michael and Dr Engin Akarlı for their translation of *On dört yıl dolandım Pervânelikte* (Fourteen years I wandered in the moth's orbit) of the poet Sıtkı (Sıtkı Baba, 1865-1928) which inspired the late Ali Ekber Çiçek to compose his version *On dört bin yıl gezdim pervanelikte* (I wandered for fourteen thousand years) exploring innovative playing techniques.

In Germany, I thank Professor Ricardo Eichmann of the Orient-Abteilung of the Deutsches Archäologisches Institut in Berlin for sharing his expertise on ancient long-necked lutes and permission to use illustrations from his publications. Dr Beate Henke, Berlin, for sending *Untersuchungen zur altmesopotamischen Laute und ihrer sozio-kulturellen Stellung*.

In Austria, I thank the luthiers Karl Kirchmeyr, Vienna, for his information about the *colascione* and permission to use the digital images of *colasciones* built by him, and Dieter Schossig, Großmehring, for sending his *Der Colascione - eine Langhalslaure in 17./18. Jahrhundert* as well as digital images of *colasciones*.

In the USA, I thank Professor W.B. Denny, for making available digital images of lutes on Ottoman miniature paintings from his extensive archive. Dr Arash Aboutorabi Hamedani, the University of Georgia, for his information about the occurrence of the name *tanbûr* in the poetry of Mevlânâ.

In Japan, I thank the Tokyo National University of Fine Arts and Music (Tōkyō Geijutsu Daguku, Japan) for sending the catalogue of the musical instruments of The Koizumi Fumio Memorial Archives. Professor Koizumi Fumio (1927-1983) collected these instruments during his travels to West Asia, Eastern Europe, Africa, America, and Oceania for ethnomusicological and organological studies.

In the Netherlands, I thank Adnan Dalkiran and Veronica Divendal of the Kulsan Foundation in Amsterdam access to their archive and images. The Plantage Library of the University of Amsterdam for making a slide of an engraving from the *Description de l'Égypt. Des instrumens à cordes connus and Égypt* by Guillaume-André Villoteau depicting various *tanbûrs*. The slide of the engraving was made by photographer Louis van der Laan (*d*. 2002),who was affiliated with the University of Amsterdam. Henny de Bruin, *Atlas of Plucked Instruments*, for his permission to use digital images of his collection. The luthier J.J. van Gool, for answering technical questions about lute construction and reading and commenting the chapter on the construction of the *bağlama*.

I thank The Walters Art Museum in Baltimore and the Freer Gallery of Art, Smithsonian Institution, in Washington, the Oxford University Press in Oxford, the Plantage Bibliotheek of the University of Amsterdam and René Gremaux in Nijmegen, the Dietrich Reimer Verlag in Berlin, the publisher Denise Harvey, the Melissa Publishing House, and the National Archaeological Museum in Greece, Jérôme Cler in France, Efrén López in Spain, Kemal Dinç in Germany, Ulaş Özdemir and the late Ergun Çağatay in Istanbul, and Yavuz Gül in Izmir for generously granting me permission to use images from their collections and/or archives.

Several people read all or parts of the manuscript and shared valuable comments and suggestions.

I would like to mention Dr Leo Plenckers from the Musicological Department of the University of Amsterdam for his invaluable contribution to the first edition of this book in 2009 being the starting point for this revised and updated version.

I'm deeply indebted to Dr Saskia Willaert of the Musical Instrument Museum (MIM) in Brussels for reading and commenting the first chapter, the luthier Engin Topuzkanamış for reading and commenting the Chapters 2-5, and Dr Martin Greve of the Orient Institut in Istanbul for reading, commenting, and editorial suggestions.

More recently museums of musical instruments in Europe started, often in a combined effort, to digitalize their collections making them accessible for scientific research and a general public. In 2009, the Musical Instruments Museum Online (MIMO) started to create a central digital resource for musical instrument collections held in European museums. To become a tool for research this digital database should furthermore be expanded to cover musical instruments worldwide as well include iconographic and literary sources.

Apparently, this book is not the definitive study of *saz*/ba*ğlama*. It has shortcomings and lacunae requiring further updates and point to areas of further research. There are still many literary and iconographic sources, particularly in Turkey, waiting for scientific research and analysis, as well as Turkish long-necked lutes in the musical instrument collections in museums and private collectors in and outside Turkey.

Istanbul, June 2020

General Introduction

The *saz/bağlama* is the core instrument of all folk musical ensembles and orchestras and a popular instrument in the *arabesk*, entertainment, and pop music in Turkey. The *saz/bağlama* also plays an important role during the ceremonies of the Alevî and Bektaşî and among the âşıks, the Anatolian wandering poet-musicians, to accompany their partly religious repertory. The *saz/bağlama* plays furthermore an important role in musical education to teach folk musical theory, notation, performance, and acoustics and instrument construction. Its importance is also demonstrated by the fact that musicians, such as Arif Sağ, Musa Eroğlu, Erdal Erzincan, Okan Murat Öztürk, Erol Parlak, and Kemal Dinç play the *saz/bağlama* as solo instrument on the national and international concert stages.[3]

The lutes of the *saz/bağlama* family are characterized by a long and narrow neck, a carved-hollowed-out or carvel-built pear or oval-shaped, and generally round-backed bowl. The origin of the Turkish long-necked lutes, which belong to a large family of long-necked lutes which are also called *tanbûrs*, is probably ancient Persia.[4] *Tanbûrs* travelled to Anatolia with the Seljuks and even maybe before, initiating a variety of long-necked lutes in Turkey.

As an initially small nomadic two-stringed lute, the *tanbûr* left considerably less literary and iconographical traces. In Turkey, contrary to Persian and especially Mughal miniature paintings which abundantly depict often beautifully ornamented *tanbûrs* in a mainly courtly and urban environment, sources are limited. Moreover, sources in rural areas in Turkey remained scarce well into the 20th century.

After the establishment of the Republic of Turkey (*Türkiye Cumhuriyeti*) in 1923, the development and establishment of a theory folk music, being a body of modal structures, instrument tunings, and rhythms inseparable linked to the *saz/bağlama*, played an important role in the creation of a cohesive and culturally unified nation state. Musicologists, composers, and musicians played, supported by politicians, ideologists, bureaucrats, and journalists, a crucial role in the political-ideological approach of Turkish folk music. It is therefore important for obvious reasons that the Turkish folk musical tradition and the *saz/bağlama*, its education as well as scientific research should emancipate from this political-ideological approach.

Since the 1960s, Turkish long-necked lutes spread to Western Europe, America, and Canada, where they are played in diaspora communities, crossover ensembles consisting of musicians with diverse backgrounds, and by multi-instrumentalists. Moreover, new *saz/bağlama* types continue to evolve due to changing musical and tonal demands made on them.

In an increasingly globalizing world in the 21st century, the musical landscape in Turkey shows a "tendency towards a disintegration of musical traditions into internationalism and multiple musical hybrids which might be described as a process of individualization. The category of

---

[3] See Zeeuw, J. de. De Turkse Langhalsluit of Bağlama; Zeeuw, J. de. Tanbûr Long-Necked Lutes along the Silk Road and beyond: 122-136.
[4] There is much misunderstanding in the West about the names 'Persia' and 'Iran.' In this study, Persia is generally used to avoid the misconception that the Persian musical culture and instruments only correspond with contemporary Iran.

individual as used here includes individual musicians, individual music pieces, individual life experiences, identities and approaches to music, individual musical projects, individual CDs and concerts, even individual concepts of music theory, conferences or research projects. Several factors lead to this development: a growing rate and importance of migration and international mobility; the increase of cross-cultural encounters and experiences; the availability of almost all Ottoman-Turkish, Anatolian and global musical styles, instruments and other musical elements via media; the opening up of identity discourses".[5] Of importance in this respect is if the *saz/bağlama* is only an instrument of a certain musical culture or if it can 'emancipate' from its cultural roots, "like the guitar from its Iberian roots", and become a musical instrument in its own right'.[6]

---

[5] Greve, M. Makamsiz: Individualization of Traditional Music on the Eve of Kemalist Turkey.
[6] See Betton, J. Die Bağlama ls Teil der Hochschulausbidung in Deutschland?, in Çiftçi, N. and M. Greve (eds). Die Bağlama in der Türkei und Europa. Erstes Bağlama-Symposium in Deutschland. Berlin, 14-15 September 2013: 315.

Chapter-1
Historical Background

The origin and early history of the *saz*/*bağlama* is largely unknown, due to the absence or scarcity of iconographic and literary sources.[1] Moreover, the oldest surviving instruments date from the 19th century. Only since the beginning of the 20th century and especially after the establishment of the Republic of Turkey, it became increasingly possible to trace the development of Turkish long-necked lutes.

Tanbûr, Saz, Bağlama

The term *tanbûr* (*tambûr*, *tembûr*), mutated by the Arabs from the Sâsânian word *tunbûr*, is applied in art, Sûfî, and folk music as a name for long-necked lutes, characterized by a long and narrow neck and a carved-hollowed-out or carvel-built pear, oval or round-shaped and generally round-backed bowl, appearing in Turkey, Azerbaijan, south-eastern Europe, the Arab countries, and Central and South Asia. These instruments, which diffused from Persia into the musical cultures along the Silk Road, are also known as *saz*/*bağlama*, *setâr*, *dotâr*, *dutâr*, *dömbra*, and *dambura*. In Turkey the word *tanbûr* is mainly used as a name for the long-necked *tanbûr* of Ottoman classical music.[2]

In the 12th century, *sâz* surfaces in the sense of musical instrument in a work by Nezâmî (1141-1209), one of the greatest Persian poets. In 14th-century Anatolia, *saz* occurs in combination with the name *iki telli* (two strings) in a poem by the Sûfî poet Kaygısız Abdal (*d*. 1415):

> Hub çalınsın odalarda *iki telli saz* ile
>> Let love be played in the rooms with a *iki telli saz*.[3]

In 15th-century Anatolia, *saz* appears in *saz şairleris* as a name for poet-musicians playing a *saz*.[4] In the same century, *saz* is mentioned in a poem by the Sûfî poet Eşrefoğlu Rûmî of Iznik (*d*. 1469):

> Gâh hânkâhta sûfîyem gâh meyhânede fâsıkam
>> Now I'm a Sûfî in the dervish convent, or a rascal in the tavern,
> Gâh raksa grub dönerem gâh sâz olub çalınuram
>> Or I twirl in the dance, or become a *saz* and am strummed.[5]

---

[1] Musical scenes and musical instruments are an important theme in the visual arts, from painting, drawing, prints, sculpture to the minor arts of furniture decoration, faïence, bookbinding, and the like. However, depictions of musical instruments are often inexact, stylized and even consciously distorted. Artists are often subject to many interferences, such as pictorial devices and the sponsors. They are, moreover, limited by his media, especially in sculpture, tools, and lack of technical understanding of instruments necessary for their exact depiction.

[2] Hassan, S.G., M. Conway, J. Baily and J. During. Tanbûr: 61. See also Zeeuw, J. de. Tanbûr Long-Necked Lutes along the Silk Road and beyond.

[3] Gazimihâl, M.R. Halk şiirlerindeki musiki izleri: 74.

[4] Reinhard, K. and U. Reinhard. Musik der Türkei. Band 2: Die Volksmusik: 89.

[5] Translation M. Köprülü in Köprülü, F.M. Early Mystics in Turkish Literature: 376.

In Ottoman lexicography, *sâz* appears in the sense of musical instrument.[6] The educated people in the Ottoman Empire did not know the word *saz*, without a 'circumflex', used by the rural population as the generic name for the long-necked lutes such as the *cura*, *bulgarı*, *tambura*, *çöğür*, *bozuk*, *tanbura*, *şarkı*, and *bağlama*, while the general term of musical instrument was referred to by the Turkish (rural) word of *çalgı* (musical instrument, from *çalmak*, to strum, to play).

Evliyâ Çelebi (1611-1682), an Ottoman intellectual and travel writer,[7] used *sâz* in the sense of musical instrument in his *Seyahatnâme* (Book of Travels, 17th century). In rural Anatolia, *saz*, without circumflex, was used – as said above – as generic name for long-necked lutes, such as the *cura*, *bulgarı*, *tambura*, *çöğür*, *bozuk*, *tanbura*, *şarkı*, and *bağlama*, while the general term of musical instrument was referred to by the Turkish (rural) word of *çalgı*. Besides having two different meanings depending on the social stratus in which the word was used, *saz* is also linked to a double name, such as *âşık sazı*, *dede sazı*, *üç telli saz*, *balta saz*, *divan sazı*, and *meydan sazı*, specifying characteristics such as the number of strings, form, size, and construction.[8]

The word *saz*, without circumflex, is since the language reforms in the 1930s included in official written language as a generic name for long-necked lutes. In the first edition of the *Türkçe Sözlük* (Turkish Dictionary) of 1945, the word *saz* is described as musical instrument or folk musical instrument with a long neck, played with a plectrum. In the 7th edition of 1983 *saz* is described as every kind of musical instrument with strings like the *bağlama*, *cura* in Turkish folk music, and in Turkish folk music specifically *saz* refers to an instrument with a long neck and strings of which the bowl is carved-out, positioned on the lap, and played with a plectrum. In the editions since 1998, *saz* is described as the general name of musical instruments with strings like the *bağlama*, *cura*, *târ* etc. in Turkish folk music, and *bağlama* is referred to as the Turkish folk music instrument with a long neck and strings of which the bowl is carved-out.9

The origin of the term *bağlama* is still unknown. It could have been derived from the verb *bağlamak* (Turkish for to bind): the tying of movable frets (*perde*, from the Persian word *parde*) around the neck or strings to the tuning pegs.[10] The term *bağlama* appeared in the second half of the 18th century in several European writings as name for a small sized long-necked lute on engravings in the *Histoire générale, critique et philologique de la musique* (1767) by Charles-Henri de Blainville (1711-1769), *Reisebeschreibung nach Arabien und andern umliegenden Ländern* (1774, 1778) by Carsten Niebuhr (1732-1815), and *Essai sur la musique ancienne et moderne* (1780) by Jean Benjamin de Laborde (1734-1794). De Blainville was the source of de Laborde.[11]

---

[6] The 'circumflex' signifies a long pronounced vowel.

[7] See for further reading Dankoff, R. and S. Kim. An Ottoman Traveller. Selections from the Book of Travels of Evliya Çelebi.

[8] Çiftçi, N. Bezeichnungen und Definitionen traditioneller Langhalslauten im Wörterbuch Türkçe Sözlük der Türkischen Sprachgesellschaft (TDK) seit 1945 du ihre Rezeption in der deutschen Sprache- und Musikforschung, in Çiftçi, N. and M. Greve (eds). Die Bağlama in der Türkei und Europa. Erstes Bağlama-Symposium in Deutschland. Berlin, 14-15 September 2013: 103-105; Kahraman-Yücel Dağlı, A. 2005. Evliyâ Çelebi Seyahatnâmesi: 637-646.

[9] Çiftçi, N. Bezeichnungen und Definitionen traditioneller Langhalslauten im Wörterbuch Türkçe Sözlük der Türkischen Sprachgesellschaft (TDK) seit 1945 und ihre Rezeption in der deutschen Sprache- und Musikforschung, in Çiftçi, N. and M. Greve (eds). Die Bağlama in der Türkei und Europa. Erstes Bağlama-Symposium in Deutschland. Berlin, 14-15 September 2013: 107-110.

[10] Cler, J. Yayla, Pastoral Life and Lutes. CD booklet The Bağlama of the Yayla: 13.

[11] Blažeković, Z. Illustrations of Musical Instruments in Jean-Benjamine de Laborde's Essai sur la musique ancienne et moderne, in Musique, Images, Instruments. Revue française d'organologie et d'iconographie musicale 15. Portraits, ballets, traités: 149.

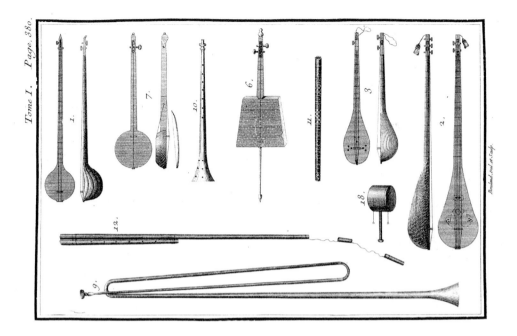

Figure 1. *Bağlama* (3), *bozuk* (2), and *iki telli* (1). Engraving *Essai sur la musique ancienne et moderne* of Jean-Benjamin de Laborde.
© Jean-Benjamin de Laborde. *Essai sur la musique ancienne et moderne*.

A few decades later we find the name *bağlama* as *tanbour baghlama* in another European writing, *Description historique, technique et littéraire des instruments de musique des orientaux* of 1823 by Guillaume-André Villoteau (1759-1839). According to the accompanying engraving, the *tanbour baghlama* was a small sized long-necked lute. Villoteau, who stayed in Cairo from 1799 until 1803 as a member of Napoleons Egyptian expedition, discussed several *tanbûrs*, played mainly by Turks, Jews, Greeks, and Armenians.[12] The dozens of scholars and artists being part of Napoleon's campaign recorded their impressions in countless drawings, paintings and publications resulting in the *Description de l'Égypte ou recueil des observations et de recherches qui ont été faites en Egypte pendant l'expédition de l'armée française, publié par les orders de sa majesté l'empereur Napoléon le Grand*, published between 1808 and 1828. These publications proved to have an enormous influence on Western European art and industry and were, moreover, for a long time an authoritative source in the field of Egyptology.

In Anatolia, the *bağlama* was also known as a small sized long-necked lute. The musicologist Sâdi Yâver Ataman (1906-1994) considered the *bozuk* as the authentic *saz* and the *cura* and *bağlama* as smaller versions of it. The musicologist Mahmut Ragıp Gazimihâl (1900-1961), on

---

[12] Villoteau, G-A. Description de l'Égypte ou recueil des observations et de recherches qui ont été faites en Egypte pendant l'expédition de l'armée française, publié par les orders de sa majesté l'empereur Napoléon le Grand. État moderne. Tome premier. Description historique, technique et littéraire des instruments de musique des orientaux. Première Partie. Des instrumens a cordes connus en Egypte. Du tanbour charqy, 265-275; Du tanbour boulghâry, 275-279; Du tanbour bouzourk, 279-287; Du tanbour baghlama, 287-290.

Figure 2. The Ottoman *tanbûr* (*tanbour kabyr tourky*) in the centre, to the left the *tanbour charqy* and the small *tanbour boulghâry*, and on the right by the *tanbour bouzourk* and the small *tanbour baghlama*. Engraving *Description de l'Égypte ou recueil des observations et de recherches qui ont été faites en Égypte* (1823) of Guillaume-André Villoteau.
© Villoteau, G-A. *Description de l'Égypte ou recueil des observations et de recherches qui ont été faites en Egypte. Des instrumens a cordes connus en Egypte*. Planches. Planche AA, Tome 2: E.M. Vol II. PL. AA.

the other hand, considered the *bağlama* as the authentic *saz*.[13] Although there is still no strict consensus about the naming *saz/bağlama*, the term *bağlama* is nowadays generally used as a generic name for Turkish long-necked lutes in Turkey.

Early and Late Antiquity

Our knowledge of ancient musical instruments is based on iconographical depictions from archaeological excavations and fragmentary artefacts of musical instruments, mostly made of wood or other easily deteriorating materials, in Mesopotamia, Egypt, Anatolia, Central Asia, India, and China. The trade routes between the Mediterranean and China stimulated the cultural interactions between these civilizations. For centuries, from antiquity to the period of Islamic history that coincided with the late Middle Ages in Europe, this arterial network of trade routes, called the Silk Road, was the most important connection between East and West. The geographical diffusion of musical instruments, as well as of other artefacts, techniques, customs, ideas etc., took place along the Silk Road trade in both directions.

The Spike Lute

The earliest representations of musical instruments were excavated in Mesopotamia in the 4th millennium BC, where the first lutes appeared on cylindrical seals towards the end of the 3rd century BC. It is likely, however, that the *spike lute* evolved earlier.[14] *Spike lutes* are rarely depicted in detail and generally only the profile of the body and the rod-shaped neck are visible. Sometimes details are depicted, such as frets, soundholes, tuning pegs, and attachments for two, three, sometimes four strings. From iconographic sources we know that the rod-shaped neck of the *spike lute* was 'woven' through a skin top, either ending within the resonator or sticking out beyond the lower end of the resonator.[15] *Spike lutes* spread along the trade networks between Mesopotamia, Egypt, and Asia Minor where they appeared on excavated archaeological sources at the latest in the 16th century BC.[16]

In Egyptian sources, one can distinguish a *spike lute* with a wooden rod-shaped neck and a tortoise shell resonator covered with a stretch skin top with soundholes, and a less common *spike bowl lute* with a wooden rod-shaped neck and a carved-hollowed-out wooden bowl covered with a stretched skin top. The strings were tied to the lower end of the rod-shaped neck and secured by ligatures wound around the top of the neck. The use of tuning pegs to tune the strings possibly dates back to the Achaemenid period (*c.* 550-331 BC). Tuning pegs became a common feature on long-necked lutes since the Hellenistic era (323-30 BC).[17]

---

[13] Ataman, S.Y. Anadolu halk sazları yerli musikiciler ve halk musiki characterleri.; Gazimihâl, M.R. Ülkelerde kopuz ve tezeneli sazlarımız.

[14] Eichman, R., P. Päffgen and N. Beyer. Lauten: 943.

[15] Eichman, R., P. Päffgen and N. Beyer. Lauten: 943-946; Eichmann, R. The Design of Ancient Egyptian Spike Lutes: 364; Wachsmann, K., *et al.* Lute: 330; Henke, B. Untersuchungen zur altmesopotamischen Laute und ihrer sozio-kulturellen Stellung: 29-30; Dinçol, B. Music and Dance among the Hittites: 582-595.

[16] Eichman, R., P. Päffgen and N. Beyer. Lauten: 943. Turnbull, H. The Origin of the Long-Necked Lute: 63-64; Bachmann, W. and B. Dinçol. Anatolia: 593.

[17] Eichmann, R. Neuaufnahme einer Schalen-Spießlaute von Deir-el-Medina (Grab 1389)/Ägypten: 7-56. A detailed and illustrated description of the construction of a 'Schalen-Spießlaut' is given by Richard Eichmann in Zwei Schalen-Spießlauten aus einer Spätzeitlichen Nekropole bei Abusir El-Meleq; Eichmann, R. Zur Konstruktion und Spielhaltung des altorientalische Spießlauten von den Anfängen bis in die seleukidisch-parthische Zeit: 589-599.

Figure 3. *Spike lute* player (bottom left) on an imprint of a cylinder seal featuring the Akkadian God of ritual and purification Ea on his throne. Akkadian cylinder seal, 2340-2284 BC.
© Trustees British Museum, London. BM 89096.

According to Henry George Farmer (1882-1965), *spike lutes* with a rod-shaped neck and a carved-hollowed-out bowl covered with a stretched skin top, such as those of Abusir el-Meleq, are the most primitive form of the *tanbûr*.[18] Ricardo Eichmann, on the other hand, believes that these lutes represent an early lute type, which were not an intermediate phase or transitional form in the general development to the so-called less 'primitive' long necked-lutes, but formed a tradition of its own.[19]

The importance of music and dance in Hittite culture in Anatolia is testified by representations on relief vases of early Hittite art on which dancers, singers, and musicians playing various musical instruments including *spike lutes* appear.[20] The characteristics of these *spike lutes* on the friezes of the famous Hittite Inandık vase (Anatolia, 16th century BC) testify that these lutes belong to the general class of ancient *spike lutes*.[21] Ceramic vases excavated in another early Hittite city, Hüseyindede, located sixty km from Inandıktepe, also depict *spike lutes* resembling those on the Inandık vase. Besides religious subjects and royal figures, they also show musicians playing castanets, cymbals, and *spike lutes*.[22] Like in Mesopotamia and Egypt, many Hittite cultic rituals were accompanied by music symbolizing divine power. Music must have, moreover, played an important role in the daily life of people as well.[23]

---

[18] Farmer, H.G. Tanbûr or Pandore: 26-28.
[19] Eichmann, R. Zwei Schalen-Spiesslauten aus einer Spätzeitlichen Nekropole bei Abusir El-Meleq: 34-35.
[20] Şare, T. Women and Music in Ancient Anatolia. The Iconographic evidence, in E. Kozal, M. Akar, Y. Heffron, Ç. Çilingirolu, T.E. Şerifoğlu, C. Çakrlar, S. Ünlüsoy and E. Jean (eds). Questions, Approaches, and Dialogues in Eastern Mediterranean Archaeology. Studies in Honor of Marie-Henriette and Charles Gates: 557.
[21] Bachmann, W. and B. Dinçol. Anatolia: 593-594.
[22] Yıldırım, T. Hüseyindede, in M. Doğan-Alparslan and M. Alparslan. Hittites. An Anatolian Empire: 228-237.
[23] Dinçol, B. Music and Dance among the Hittites, in M. Doğan-Alparslan and M. Alparslan. Hittites. An Anatolian Empire: 582-592.

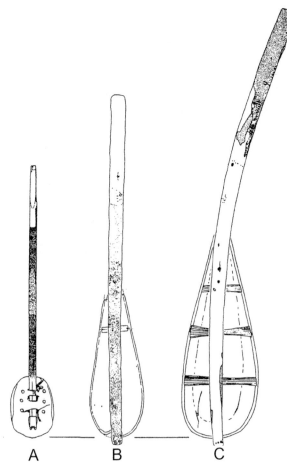

Figure 4. Drawing of an excavated Egyptian *spike tortoise shell lute* (A) from Deir el-Medina, *c.* 15th century BC, and two *spike bowl lutes* (B and C) from Abusir el-Meleq, *c.* 8th century BC.
© Courtesy Eichmann, R. *The Design of Ancient Egyptian Spike Lutes*, modified figure 1, page 368.

A   B   C

Spike lutes with a long slender rod-shaped neck, ligatures ending in decorative tassels, and very small pear or oval-shaped resonators are also represented on late Hittite iconography, such as a relief from Carchemish (Karkamış) and a orthostat relief (a stone slab set at the base of a wall) from Zincirli (south-east Anatolia, *c.* 9th-8th BC).[24] Objects, in particular those found in 1982 in a late 14th century shipwreck discovered near Uluburun (Grand Cape), south-east of Kaş, testify that there was an extensive network of trade routes between the Middle East and the Aegean region. Among the cargo were tortoise-shell bodies of *spike lutes*, indicating the diffusion of *spike lutes* from the Middle East to Anatolia.

The Necked Lute

In addition to the *spike lute*, a different type of lute, the so-called necked lute, evolved during the Seleucid-Parthian era (*c.* 323 BC - 224 AD). *Spike lutes* and necked lutes differ from each other by the way in which the neck and resonator are assembled. While the neck of the spike

---

[24] Bachmann, W. and B. Dinçol. Anatolia: 593, 597-598. Curt Sachs and Richard Campbell classified the instrument of a lute player from Zincirli as a tanbûr. This postulation is rejected by Ricardo Eichmann according to whom the lute is unidentifiable. Ricardo Eichmann. Personal communication.

Figure 5. Inandık vase, Central Anatolia, 16th century
BC (left). Detail *spike* lute player (middle). Drawing *spike*
lute player (right).
© Author, Ankara Archaeological Museum, Ankara.
© Yapı Kredi Yayınları, Istanbul. Doğan-Alparslan, M.
and M. Alparslan (eds). *Hititler. Bir Anadolu Imparatorluğu*:
369, 588.

lute passes diametrically through the resonator, the neck of the necked lutes is carved from or attached to the resonator. According to iconographical sources, the neck and resonator of the long as well as short-necked lutes, were initially carved from one single block of wood (one-piece design). Whether or not necked lutes were already present in the late Hittite period remains questionable.[25]

Long-necked lutes appear in Greek art after Alexander the Great's Persian campaigns and it is therefore quite possible that they were imported from Persia or Asia Minor.[26] They are shown in the hands of terracotta figurines and a Muse on a marble relief. The more common type had an oval-shaped resonator converging into the neck, whereas the less common type had a spade-shaped resonator with a straight lower end and a triangular-shaped back converging towards the neck of which the top suggests the presence of tuning pegs.[27]

The Persian conquest was a turning point in the civilizations of Asia Minor (Anatolia). Between 547-337 BC, Anatolia was part of the Achaemenid Empire (*c.* 550-331 BC) followed by the Hellenistic era after the conquest of Alexander the Great (336-323 BC). Since 301, Asia Minor

[25] Wachsmann, K. *et al.* Lute: 329-331; Eichmann, R. Zur Konstruktion und Spielhaltung der Altorientalische Spiesslautenvond den Anfängen bis in die Seleukidisch-Parthische Zeit: 621.
[26] Bachmann, W. and B. Dinçol. Anatolia, § 5 (iv): Western Anatolia: Lydian period (c. 678-547/ BCE): 602; Higgins, R.A and R.D. Winnington-Ingram. Lute-players in Greek Art: 62, 68; Mathiesen, T.J. Apollo's Lyre. Greek Music and Music Theory in Antiquity and the Middle Ages: 204, 284.
[27] Higgins, R.A. and R.D. Winnington-Ingram. Lute-players in Greek Art: 63-64; See Mathiesen, T.J. Apollo's Lyre: 284; West, M.L. Ancient Greek Music: 283-286; Eichmann, R. Koptische Lauten. Eine musikalische Untersuchung von sieben Langhalslauten des 3.-9. Jahrhunderts aus Egypten: 94.

Figure 6. Draped female playing a *pandoura*. Cyprus figurine, late 4th century BC (left). Draped female playing a *pandoura*. To her left, a women is holding an *aulos*. Marble relief Mantineia temple built in honour of Leto and her children Apollo and Artemis, 330-320 BC (right).
© Author, British Museum, London. BM 1919.6-20.7.
© Courtesy National Archaeological Museum, Athens. Inv. nr. 216.

was for almost a century part of the Seleucid Empire (312-129 BC) stretching from Thrace in Europe to the border of India. Whether or not necked lutes were present in Anatolia during Achaemenid, Hellenistic or Seleucid times is unknown.

A puzzling terracotta from the Seleucid era, representing a draped female lute player, raises the question whether the incised two lines on the bowl refer to the lower part of the neck of a *spike lute* or to the two strings of a long-necked lute carved from a single block of wood.[28] If the latter is the case, the Seleucid terracotta belongs, together with the lute player on the Mantinea relief and the lute playing Cyprus figurine, to the earliest iconographical representations of long-necked lutes predating the appearance of the Sâsânian long-necked *tunbûr* in literary and iconographic sources of the 5th-7th centuries.[29]

The Sâsânian Tunbûr

Iconographical and literary sources of the Sâsânian era (*c*. AD 224-651) testify that music and musical instruments played an important role at the Persian Sâsânian courts and contributed

---

[28] Eichmann, R. Zur Konstruktion und Spielhaltung des altorientalische Spießlauten von den Anfängen bis in die seleukidisch-parthische Zeit: 608.
[29] The images of lutes from 3rd-1st millennium BC do not allow to distinguish clearly different construction types. What is attested until the Hellensitic period of Mesopotamia, is the presence of spike lutes (2nd/3rd millennium BC). Necked lutes appeared during the Hellenistic period. They may have already been in use in earlier times, but this cannot be proved yet. To my knowledge, it is still unknown where necked lutes (like the tanbûr) emerged. Moreover, there may have been evolutionary or transitional forms, of tanbûr-like instruments, which were neither a spike nor a necked-lute. I speculated about a Central Asian origin and its dispersal to the west (under Alexander the Great), but this is not attested. Ricardo Eichmann. Personal communication.

Figure 7. Female torso with a *spike lute*, 312 BC-AD 129 (left). Female torso with a lute of which the two incised lines on the pear-shaped resonator could be the lower part of the rod-shaped neck of a *spike lute* or, although debatable, the two strings of a necked lute, 312 BC-AD 129 (right).
© Iraq Museum, Baghdâd. Inv. nr. 72736.
© Staatlichen Museen, Vorderasiatisches Museum, Berlin. VAB Bab 345.

to their splendour. *Tunbûr* as the name for a long-necked lute probably appeared for the first time on 5th-century text fragments in Pahlahwî, the official language of the Sâsânians, and on two Sâsânian plates (5th-7th century), testifying that the long-necked *tunbûr* belonged, together with the short-necked *barbât* to the musical instruments played at the Sâsânian courts.[30]

Besides scholars, the court of Šâpûr I (r. 239/240-272) at Bishâpûr attracted also musicians from India. They not only introduced their performing practices and playing techniques, but also brought their musical instruments with them. The legend goes that the *barbât* was invented during the reign of Šâpûr I. Henry George Farmer supposed, however, that the ancestor of the *barbât* was introduced from India or Afghanistan during his reign.[31] Although there is virtually no evidence to support the hypothesis of an Indian or Afghan ancestor of the *tunbûr*, it seems not unreasonable to consider an Afghan ancestry.

The *tunbûr* on a Sâsânian silver plate from the Freer Gallery of Art in Washington is depicted in more detail than the *tunbûr* on a silver plate now in the State Historical Museum in Moscow, the so-called Alkino silver plate; only the outline of the tunbûr is depicted. The neck of both

---

[30] Lawgren, B., A. Farhat and S. Blum. Iran: 522, 528-529.
[31] (Barbât) '......soll der Überlieferung zufolge während der Regierungszeit Šâpûr I (241-272) erfunden worden sein. Es ware warscheinlich korrekter, wenn man annimt, daß die schlanke Kurzhalslaute in dieser Zeit aus Indien und Afghanistan nach Persien eingeführt wurde'. Farmer, H.G. Islam. Musikgeschichte in Bildern. Musik des Mittelalters under Renaissance:: 18, 106; Farmer, H.G. The Origin of the Arabian Lute and Rebec. Journal of the Royal Asiatic Society 62: 767-783; Garthwaite, G.R. The Persians: 92.

Figure 8. Sâsânian silver plate showing a poet-musician playing a *tunbûr*, 5th–7th centuries AD. Clearly visible the small soundholes in the skin top or wooden soundboard and the two dorsally positioned wooden 'pins' or tuning pegs in the top of the neck to secure and/or tune the strings, probably tied to a crescent-shaped bridge.
© Courtesy Freer Gallery of Art, Smithsonian Institution, Washington, D.C.: Purchase – Charles Lang Freer Endowment. F1964.10.

tunbûrs converges without a clear demarcation into the bowl, indicating that they were carved from a single block of wood. Their necks show no traces of frets, which may have been a matter of simplified representation.[32] The clearly visible two strings of the *tunbûr* on the silver plate of the Freer Gallery of Art seem to be attached to a crescent-shaped bridge, positioned on a stretched skin top or wooden soundboard with small soundholes, and tied to two wooden pins or pegs in the top of the neck to secure and/or tune the strings.[33]

The *tunbûr* was most probably played with the fingers of the right hand, since no plectrum is represented between the thumb and the index finger on iconographical sources. A plectrum was probably not used on the *tunbûr*, mutated by the Arabs to *tanbûr*, before the 8th century. According to Henry George Farmer, the *tanbûr* did have movable frets tied around the neck. Frets were used by the Egyptians, but not by the Greeks and the Arabs before the 8th century.[34]

---

[32] The use of iconography is often debated. Were the artists' models accurate? Which elements of the illustrations are imaginary and which are real? To what extent were artists obliged or even limited by the contemporary style and or demands of their patron? Moreover, the depiction of musical instruments requires certain skills.

[33] Karomatov, F.M, V.A. Meškeris and T.S. Vyzgo. Mittelasien: 62-63. Contemporary texts document the practice of presenting such royal vessels as gifts. Since at least as early as the 4th century the official production was imitated beyond the borders of ancient Persia by rulers who chose to model their courts on the Achaemenid and Sâsânian courts like the Alkino silver plate (Freer Gallery of Art).

[34] Djani-Zade, T. Die organologische und ikonographische Gestalt der türkischen Lauten. Über das historische Zupfinstrument qâpâz-i ôz: 71; Farmer, H.G. Was the Arabian and Persian Lute Fretted? Al-Farâbî, Abu Nasr. Kitâb al-Mûsîqî al-Kabîr; Wright, O. (ed.). On Music: An Arabic critical edition and English translation of Epistle 5 (Epistles of the Brethren of Purity); Sawa, G.D. Music Performance Practice in the Early cAbbâsid Era 132-320 AH / 750-932 AD: 81-83; Zeeuw, J. de. Tanbûr Long-Necked Lutes along the Silk Road and beyond: 12-14.

The Umayyad and Abbâsid Tanbûrs

The Persian *tanbûr* arrived at the Umayyad court in Damascus in the 2nd half of the 7th century with the singing girls which were 'imported' from Khurâsân, an ancient region encompassing contemporary north-eastern Iran, southern Turkmenistan, and northern Afghanistan. Initially, the *tanbûr* belonged to the most favourite instruments at the Abbâsid court in the 8th century before the *'ûd* became the leading instrument of court and urban music as well as the instrument preferred by theorists to demonstrate the modal structures of the Arabic *maqâm*.[35]

The development of the *tanbûr* was influenced by the *'ûd*, the immediate ancestor of the European classical lute, which evolved in the 7th/8th century. In the course of time more frets and strings, sometimes doubled or tripled, were added. The extension of the number of frets made it possible to play the larger melodic range of the *maqâm*-based music. The composite design of the *'ûd*, according to which the neck is attached to the bowl, was in time also applied to the *tanbûr*. Moreover, a new playing technique with a plectrum was introduced. These developments mainly took place in a courtly and urban environment and resulted in larger sophisticated *tanbûrs*.[36]

The *tanbûrs* discussed by Abu Nasr al-Farâbî (*c.* 870-*c.* 950) in the 10th century in his *Kitâb al-Mûsîqî al-Kabîr* (Great Book of Music), the *tanbûr al-baghdâdî* and the *tanbûr al-khurasânî*, were fretted. According to their fretting, they must have been instruments of art music and not of folk music. Unlike the *'ûd*, these *tanbûrs* did not belong to the inner circle of the instruments of the court and urban *maqâm* tradition of Umayyad Damascus and Abbâsid Baghdâd.

The Rum-Seljuks

The diffusion of *tanbûrs* from the Persian domain into the musical cultures along the Silk Road resulted in a variety of long-necked lutes with bowls in various shapes, two or more, occasionally doubled or tripled courses, a varying number of different tuned frets and strings each having its own characteristic sound, playing technique (with the fingers, a plectrum, the nail of the index finger, a thimble-pick plectrum on the index finger or a bow), and repertory.[37]

Between the 9th and the 12th century, various independent Turco-Persian Islamic dynasties overran the eastern provinces of the Abâssid Empire (750-1258), Khurâsân ('Land of the Sun'), and Transoxiana ('Land behind the Oxus'), where the Tâhirids (821-873), the Sâmânids (819-999), and the Bûwayhids (954-1055) initiated a revival of the ancient Persian language and culture. The Turco-Persian civilization spread westwards with the Seljuks, a conglomerate of Turkish tribes and clans, the so-called Oğhuz.

The ancestor of the Turkish long-necked lutes, the *tanbûr*, probably reached Anatolia during the Seljuq conquest at the latest in the 11th century. The only available evidence of the presence of necked lutes in Anatolia before the Seljuk conquest is a three-stringed fretless lute (*pandoura?*) on a 5th-century Byzantine mosaic of which the bowl was probably covered with a skin top.[38]

---

[35] Wegner, U. 'Ûd: 1089-1102.
[36] During, J. Dotâr. Iran, Central Asia and Anatolia: 83; Djani-Zade, T. Die organologische und ikonographische Gestalt der türkischen Lauten. Über das historische Zupfinstrument qâpâz-i ôz: 71.
[37] Bachmann, W. Die Anfänge des Streichinstrumentenspiels.
[38] Picken, L. Folk Musical Instruments of Turkey: 263.

Whether neck lutes were present before the 11th century, and if so, whether these instruments contributed to the further development of long-necked lutes in Anatolia, will probably remain unknown due to the absence of literary and iconographic sources.[39]

The court of the Rum-Seljuks in Konya, being one of the thriving cultural centres in the Islamic world, attracted scholars, poets, and musicians. Especially at the court of Sultan Alâ al-Dîn Kayqubâd I (r. 1219-1237), a well-known patron of literature and poetry, music took an important place. The Seljuk rulers received a literary education and were familiar with Persian poetry. Some of them were poets themselves overloading the court poets with favours.

The influence of the Persian civilization on the Turks dates from the time of the last Sâsânid rulers, especially after the Persians converted to Islam. Under the Anatolian Turco-Persian Seljuks, court life, politics, and the arts were heavily indebted to the Persian culture. The Persian musical praxis and musical instruments, among which *tanbûrs*, must also have been an example for the Turks of Anatolia since Seljuk times.[40]

The Persian influence is also attested by the excavated 'minai'i' ceramic tiles from the summer palace of Sultan Alâ al-Dîn Kayqubâd I, the Kubadabad Sarayı, located on the southwest shores of lake Beyşehir west of Konya. The Persian so-called mina'i technique (Persian for 'enamel) was also used for the ceramic tiles made in Seljuq Anatolia.[41] One of the excavated tiles shows a cross-seated *ozan* (poet-musician) probably playing a probably two-stringed *tanbûr* and resembling the poet-musician with the *tunbûr* on the Freer Gallery of Art Sâsânian silver plate. Some Seljuk rulers were passionate lovers of music and it seems therefore reasonable to suppose that poet-musicians must have been important guests at the Seljuk courts.

The common people, however, remained strangers to the cultivated Persian cultural traditions of the Anatolian centres. The *ozans* wandered from campsite to campsite, performing Oğhuz epics and heroic poems at public or private gatherings (of which only the *Dede Korkut Kitabı* still gives an idea), or popular folk songs about contemporary events accompanied by the *kopuz*. They may also have performed magic or done fortune telling. They were present at national hunting rites (*sığır*) and at mourning ceremonies (*yoğ*) and travelled with the Seljuk army performing heroic poetry after military victories.[42] The Anatolian Turks possessed a large body of love poems and folk songs such as the *türkü*, *türkmânî*, and *varsağı*, revealing the ethnic nature of the Oğhuz Turks, or *koşma*, *deyiş* or *kayabaşı*, and demonstrating their rustic nature or requirement of musical accompaniment. Unfortunately almost nothing is left of these epics, heroic and love poems, and folk songs.[43]

The first references to lutes in Anatolian texts can be found in the work of the poet-mystic Yûnus Emre (1249-1322). He mentions the *kopuzıla çeşte* (*kopuz* with six strings) and the *kopuz*

---

[39] Zeeuw, J. de. De Turkse Langhalsluit of Bağlama: 33.
[40] Köprülü, M.F. Early Mystics in Turkish Literature: 9, 218-220n7, 11, 12; Song Creators in Eastern Turkey. Reinhard, U. CD-Booklet: 3; Feldman, M. Music of the Ottoman Court. Makam, Composition and the Early Ottoman Instrumental Repertoire: 449: see also Uslu, R. Selçuklu Topraklarında Müzik.
[41] Ertuğ, A. 1991. The Seljuks. A Journey Through Anatolian Architecture: 38-40; Sims, E. 2002. Peerless Images. Persian Painting and its Sources. 33-36; Canby, S.R., D. Beyazit, M. Rugladi and A.C.S. Peacock. Court and Cosmos: The Great Age of the Seljuks. 160-161; Sims, E. Peerless Images. Persian Painting and its Sources: 36.
[42] Köprülü, M.F. Early Mystics in Turkish Literature: 3.
[43] Köprülü, F.M. Early Mystics in Turkish Literature: 210-211.

Figure 9. Poet-musician playing a *tanbûr* in the usual cross-seated playing position of Central Asia with the neck pointed downwards like the *tanbûr* players on the Sâsânian silver plates. Six-pointed star tile ensemble excavated at the summer palace of Sultan Alâ al-Dîn Kayqubâd I, Anatolia, early 13th century. © Museum für Islamische Kunst, Staatliche Museen, Berlin. Inv. nr. 00026603.

or *kolca kopuz* (*kopuz* with an arm, =neck) in the *Dede Korkut Kitabı*, partly covered with a skin top. The word *kopuz* probably appears for the first time in the *Divân Lughât al-turk* (Dictionary of the Turkish languages, 1072-1083) of the Uyghur scholar Mahmud al-Kâshgarî. According to al-Kâshgarî, the *kopuz* resembles the *'ûd*, an indication that the *kopuz* must have been a short-necked lute.[44]

The orally transmitted stories of the *Dede Korkut Kitabı* date from the 10th/11th century, the published version from the 16th century. The legend of Dede Korkut was known on the banks of the Syr Darya, the old territory of the Oğhuz, among Turkmen, around Derbend in Azerbaijan, in Anatolia, in short, all the areas to which branches of the Oğhuz spread. In the western version, Dede Korkut appears as a wise spiritual man, an adviser of khâns, a leader of the Muslims, in the eastern version as a *shaman* controlling the powers of nature. For the Azerbaijani and Turks the *kopuz* was a plucked lute, for the Uzbeks, Kazakhs, Kyrgyz, and Karakalpaks and Kalmyks a fiddle.[45]

According to the music theorist Abd al-Qâdir Ibnu Ghaibî al-Marâghî (d. 1435), a famous composer and musician in his time, the Oğhuz Turks used the word *kopuz* for strummed lutes before Ottoman times. Regarding his own time, al-Marâghî, who spent some time at the court of Sultan Beyâzîd I (r. 1389-1402), distinguished two *kopuz* types, the *kopuz-i ozan* (the lute of the travelling poet-musicians, the *ozan*) and the *kopuz-i rûmî* (the Turkish or Byzantine *kopuz*). The bowl of the first was partially covered with a skin top and had three gut strings. The bowl

---

[44] Picken, L. Folk Musical Instruments of Turkey: 265; Djani-Zade, T. 2004. Die organologische und ikonographische Gestalt der türkischen Lauten. Über das historische Zupfinstrument qâpâz-i ôz: 77.
[45] Köprülü, F.M. Early Mystics in Turkish Literature: 15-16; Djani-Zade, T. 2004. Die organologische und ikonographische Gestalt der türkischen Lauten. Über das historische Zupfinstrument qâpâz-i ôz: 74; Picken, L. Musical Instruments of Turkey: 267: The small size of the kopuz is suggested by the lines in the Dede Korkut Kitabı Gördi kim bilinde kopuzı var (He saw that he had a kopuz at his waist), which could be an indication of a small fiddle.

Figure 10. Replica of the *qolça qopuz*, length 81 cm, length bowl 41 cm and 24 cm wide, by Mejnun Kerimov. © Yeni Nasıl Publishing House, Baku, Azerbaijan. Kerimov, M. *The Azerbaijan Musical Instruments*. Illustration 24, page 63.

of the second was completely covered with a skin top and had five two-string courses which were also made of gut.[46]

A replica of the *kolca kopuz* (*qolça qopuz*) by the musicologist Majnun Kerimov from Baku resembles al-Marâghî's description of the *kopuz-i ozan*: 'The bowl of it is longer than the bowls of all other instruments, and over half the surface they stretch skin, and on it they tie three single strings'. Kerimov 'recreated' various traditional musical instruments, primarily based on literary and iconographic sources, such as the *choghur*, *Shirvan tanbur*, *saz*, and *kopuz*. A Byzantine instrument from the 10th/11th, century excavated in Corinth, seems in agreement with al-Marâghî's description of the *kopuz-i rûmî*: 'This is an instrument the bowl and the belly of which are carved out of a piece wood; and on the surface they stretch a skin and tie five double strings on it'.[47]

The skin top links the *kopuz* to the *rabâb* (*rubâb*, *rebab*, *rawab*), a generic name for various plucked or bowed lutes, mainly with a skin top. The most important difference between the *rabâb* and *tanbûr* is that the first is a lute whose bowl is partially or completely covered with a skin top and whose neck is generally fretless neck, while the latter has a bowl with a wooden top and a long and usually fretted neck.[48]

Although some authors suppose the *kopuz* to be the ancestor of the *saz/bağlama*, the available iconographic and literary sources contradict this hypothesis. The long-necked *tanbûr*, emphasizing the influence of the Persian musical culture on the Anatolian Seljuks, and not the *kopuz* is the ancestor of the Turkish long-necked lutes. The Turkey, the term *kopuz* is in still used by musicians and luthiers as a name for Turkish long-necked lutes.[49]

The word *tanbûr* appeared several times in the poetry of the mystics and Sûfî poet Mevlânâ Celâlü'ddîn Rûmî (d. 1273), probably the greatest and most influential representative of pantheism in Persian Sûfî poetry.[50] Music played an important

[46] Picken, L. Folk Musical Instruments of Turkey: 266; Feldman, W. Music of the Ottoman Court. Makam, Composition and the Early Ottoman Instrumental Repertoire: 117.

[47] Picken, L. Folk Musical Instruments of Turkey: 265-267; Kerimov, N. The Azerbaijan Musicl Instrument: 120-148.

[48] Dick, A., C. Poché, J.P. Baker Dobbs, M.J. Kartomi, J. During and J. Baily. Rabâb: 696-702.

[49] Gazimihâl, M.R. Ülkelerde Kopuz ve Tezeneli Sazlarımız; Elderova, E. 'Saz – Osnovnoij muzykal'nye instrument azerbajdžanskoy SSR; Parlak, E. Türkiye'de el ile (şelpe) bağlama çalma geleneği ve çalış teknikleri; Feldman, W. Music of the Ottoman Court. Makam, Composition and the Early Ottoman Instrumental Repertoire: 508-509, n46; Djani-Zade, T. 2004. Die organologische und ikonographische Gestalt der türkischen Lauten. Über das historische Zupfinstrument qâpâz-i ôz.

[50] See for short biography Köprülü, M.F. D Jalâl a-Dîn Rûmî, in M.F. Köprülü. Early Mystics in Turkish Literature: 201-204.

role in the thinking of Rûmî'. Musical instruments, such as the *ney*, the *rabâb*, and the *tanbûr*, are vehicles to reveal and express deeper spiritual meanings. In his *Divân*, the word *tanbûr* occurred ten times and the *rabâb* no less than fifty-five times. In the *Masnavî-yi Ma'navî* (Rhymed Couplets of Spiritual Meaning), often referred to as 'the Qur'an in Persian', the word *rabâb* occurred several times, whereas the *tanbûr* was mentioned only once in the fourth book. The story goes that Rûmî himself played the bowed *rabâb*.[51]

The Karaman court poet Aynî (15th century),[52] who fused Sûfî and secular ideas of music in his poetry, also mentions the *tanbûr*, besides other instruments such as the *rubâb*, the *'ûd*, the *santûr*, the *kanûn*, and the *kemân*, several times. In one of his poems he emphasizes the *tanbûr* as an instrument revealing divine mysteries. The use of musical imagery and names of musical instruments was one of the mystical components of in Sûfî and/or Divân poetry since Mevlânâ.

The Anatolian Long-Necked Lutes

Miniature paintings from the Trebizond Alexander Romance, a 14th century Byzantine Anatolian illustrated manuscript on the life and works of Alexander the Great, pre-dating al-Marâghî, show two and three-stringed long-necked lutes with an ovoid or round-shaped bowl and angled pegbox (*pandouras?*). Unknown is if these lutes played a role in the development of Turkish long-necked lutes in Anatolia. The manuscript, famous for its countless refined miniatures, was ordered by the Byzantine emperor of Trebizond (Trabzon) Alexios III Komnenos (1349-1390) for his personal library and came in Turkish hands In 1461, after the conquest of Trebizond by Sultan Mehmed II (*r*. 1451-1481). It is unknown if the lutes represented in the miniatures influenced the development of Turkish long-necked lutes in Anatolia.[53]

Possible links in the development of long-necked lutes in Anatolia are the *tanbûr-i şirvânîyân* (the *tanbûr* of Shirwân, located in the north of Azerbaijan) and the *tanbûre-i türkî* (the *tanbûr* of the Turks), discussed by Abd al-Qâdir al-Marâghî in the early 15th century. Compared to the *tanbûre-türkî*, the *tanbûr-i şirvânîyân* had a smaller pear-shaped bowl, a longer neck, and two (*iki telli*) or three strings (*üç telli*). In the 15th century, the Turks possibly added a string that served as a bourdon, a fixed fundamental continuous tone sounding simultaneously with the melody (*dem sesi*).[54] In the same century, the word *saz* appeared in Anatolia as a name for the lute of the poet-musicians, the *saz şairleris*, 'poets with a *saz*', which was probably a generic name for long-necked lutes.

Ottoman 15th-century musical sources testify that *tanbûrs* initially were included in court ensembles. Tursun Bey (*c.* 1426-*c.* 1491) describes in his history of the reign of Sultan Mehmed II, the *Târîh-i Ebü'l-Feth*, the circumcision festivities held in a tent on an island in the Maritza river at Edirne in 1457 for prince Bayezid and prince Mustafa, the sons of Sultan Mehmed II.

---

[51] Arash Aboutorabi Hamedani. Personal communication; Schimmel, A. Mystical Dimensions of Islam: 317-318, 324-325.

[52] The Karaman state, the Karamanoğulları Beyliği (2nd half 13th century-1487) was a powerful beylik, principalities which emerged after the collapse of the Rum Seljuk and Mongol power, with the former Rum Seljuk capital Konya as their capital. McCarthy J. The Ottoman Turks. An introductory History to 1923: 36; Inalcık, H. The Ottoman Empire. The Classical Age 1300-1600: 14.

[53] Anoyanakis, F. Greek Popular Musical Instruments: 22-23, 38, 212; Kastritsis D. The Trebizond Alexander Romance (Venice Hellenic Institute Codex Gr. 5): The Ottoman Fate of a Fourteenth-Century Illustrated Byzantine Manuscript: 103-104.

[54] Abd al-Qâdir Ibnu Ghaibî al-Marâghî. Maqâsid al-Alhân.

Figure 11. Long-necked lutes (*pandouras?*) on two miniature paintings from the *Romance of Alexander the Great*. Trabzon, northern Anatolia, 14th century.
© Hellenic Institute of Byzantine and Post-Byzantine Studies, Venice. *Romance of Alexander the Great.*
F 49 v, f 75 r.

The use of the term '*kânun-i pâdîşâhî*' indicates musical entertainment at the Ottoman court. Tursun Bey describes an ensemble comprising of instruments such as the '*ûd, şeştar, tanbûr, rebâb, barbût*, and *nây*.[55]

According to the famous Ottoman biographer *Aşık* Çelebi (*d.* 1571) in his *Meşâ'ir* üş-Şu'arâ (Lives of the Poets, 1568), the Ottoman prince Korkut (1467-1513), governor of Amasya and a poet, composer, and musician attracted towards Sûfîsm, invented a *tanbûr* called *rûh-efzâ* or *gıdâ-yi rûh* ('food of soul or spirit').[56] The *rûh-efzâ*, possibly an Anatolian version of the by al-Marâghî cited *rûh-efzâ*, was probably one of the *tanbûrs* of Ottoman classical music in the 15th century, which were excluded from the Ottoman courtly ensembles in the 16th century.[57]

The Ottoman Empire

In the 16th century, most countries of the Near East, Persia, Asia Minor, and parts of India were ruled by three major Islamic empires, the so-called 'Gunpowder Empires', the Ottomans in Asia Minor, the Safavids in Persia, and the Mughals in India. The Turko-Persian legacy, which reached its zenith in the 16th century, was reinforced by the circulation of people along the protected trade routes between Istanbul, Isfahan, and Delhi.[58] Besides merchants, scholars, philosophers, and poets, ideas about music, musicians, and musical instruments travelled along these trade routes across political and cultural boundaries. Besides travelling musicians with their instruments, travelling or captured instrument makers. They must have contributed

---

[55] Tursun Bey (Tulum, M. ed.). Târîh-i Ebü'l-Feth: 90; Pekin, E. Sultan Bestekârlar: 21; Feldman, W. Music of the Ottoman Court. Makam, Composition and the Early Ottoman Instrumental Repertoire. 494.
[56] Feldman, W. Music of the Ottoman Court. Makam, Composition and the Early Ottoman Instrumental Repertoire: 143.
[57] Feldman, W. Music of the Ottoman Court. Makam, Composition and the Early Ottoman Instrumental Repertoire: 144-145.
[58] Dale, S.F. The Muslim Empires of the Ottomans, Safavids, and Mughals: 3.

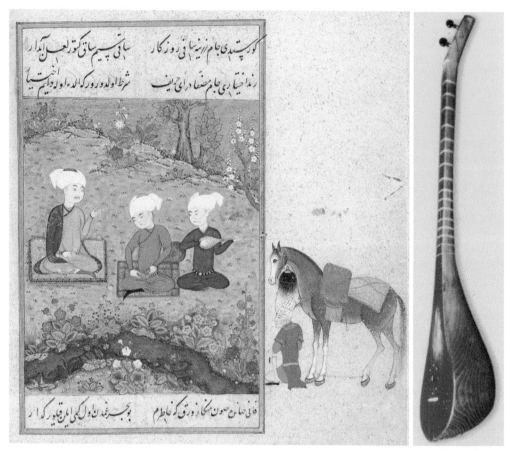

Figure 12. Tîmûrid prince in a blossoming landscape drinking wine while being entertained by a singer accompanied by a musician playing a small two-stringed *tanbûr* (*tanbûr-i şirvânîyân?*), probably Tabriz, *c.* 1478 (left). Replica of the two-stringed *tanbûr-i şirvânîyân* by Majnun Kerimov, 1982 (right).
© Chester Beatty Library, Dublin. CBL T 401, folio 8v.
© Yeni Nasıl Publishing House, Baku, Azerbaijan. Kerimov, M. *The Azerbaijan Musical Instruments*.
Illustration 31, page 78.

to the distribution of construction techniques of musical instruments among which those of *tanbûrs*.

The conquest of Istanbul in 1453 by the Ottoman army was the final blow to the Byzantine Empire. The period that began with the reign of Sultan Mehmed II and ended with the reign of Sultan Süleyman I (Kanunî, 'the Lawgiver', 1520-1566), is considered to be the 'Classical Age' of the Ottoman Empire reaching its largest territorial size in the 17th century. The siege of Vienna by the Ottomans in 1683 resulted in their defeat marking the end of their domination in eastern Europe.

Music played an important role at the Ottoman courts which were initially strongly influenced by the Persian musical culture. Especially during the time of Sultan Selim I (Yavuz, 'the

Figure 13. Bird-eye view of Istanbul and the Bosporus by M.M. Rourague Frères (1855) with on the foreground the Topkapı Sarayı, on the other side of the Golden Horn Galata, to the right Üsküdar, and on the background the Black Sea.
© EKAV /Eğitim Kültür ve Araştırma Vakfı, Istanbul. Cezar, M. *Osmanlı Başkenti Istanbul*: 283.

Terrible', *r.* 1512-1520) and Sultan Süleyman I (*r.* 1520-1566) modelled their court on that of the Persian Safavids (1502-1736), a dynasty based on an alliance of Turkish tribes west of Persia. Süleyman I, whose taste for luxury won him the epithet 'Magnificent' in Europe, grew in his late fifties more scrupulous about religion. The Venetian ambassador in Istanbul between 1550 and 1552, Bernardo Navagero (1507-1565), reported that the sultan had given up drinking wine and listening to music and accordingly ordered to burn the musical instruments of the Topkapı Sarayı.[59]

A miniature painting from the *Süleymanname* (Book of Süleyman, 1588), covering the historical events from 1520 to 1555, shows Süleyman I and his son Şehzade Mustafa (1515-1553), during their meeting in Kayseri in 1548.[60] One of the musicians on the foreground (bottom left) is playing a long-necked (?) lute[61] with an long and oval-shaped plectrum. A miniature painting

---

[59] Report made by Bernardo Navagaro to the Republic of Venice. See Bernardo Navagero, 'Relazione dell'Impero Ottomano del Clarissimo Bernardo Navagero, Stato Bailo a Costantinopoli Fatta in Pregadi nel Mese di Febbrajo del 1553,' in Relazioni degli Ambasciatori Veneti al Senato, ed. Eugenio Albèri, III, v.1: 72–73.
[60] In 1548 Süleyman joined the Ottoman Army against the Safavids. The popular Şehzade Mustafa, his first born son by haseki Mahidevran Gülbahar Sultan who was meant to be the heir to the Ottoman throne. Süleyman's wife haseki Hürrem (1500?-1558) probably conspired with her grandson Rüstem Pasha to kill Mustafa in favor of her son Selim. Mustafa was killed with a silken rope.
[61] There are forms to which neither label – short or long – applies well.

Figure 14. Sultan Süleyman I and his son Şehzade Mustafa (1515-1553). *Süleyman Conversing with Mustafa, Süleymanname* (1588). On the foreground musicians playing a three-stringed long-necked lute (*tanbûr*) with a long tortoise shell plectrum and a *tambourine* (left). Prince in a courtyard entertained by musicians playing a three-stringed long-necked lutes (*tanbûrs*) and a *def. Entertainment in a palace courtyard* from an illustrated copy of the *Divân-i Nevâ'î* (c. 1530) of Mir 'Alî Shîr Nevâ'î (right).
© Topkapı Sarayı Müzesi, Istanbul. *Divân-i Nevâ'î*. H. 1517, folio 477b.
© Topkapı Sarayı Müzesi, Istanbul. *Süleymanname*. R. 804, folio 111b.

from a copy of the *Divân-i Nevâ'î, Entertainment in a palace courtyard*, illustrated by artists from Tabrîz in an Ottoman studio around 1530, shows a prince entertained by musicians playing a *def* and three-stringed long-necked lutes (*tanbûrs*). The *tanbûr* was among other instruments mentioned in the *Divân-i Nevâ'î* by the Turkish poet and scholar Mir 'Alî Shîr Nevâ'î (Herât, 1441-1501), who stayed until 1481 at the brilliant court of the last Tîmûrid Sultan Husayn Mîrzâ Bayqarâ (r. 1469-1506).[62]

---

[62] Çalka, M.S. 2008. Nev'î Divânı'nda Mûsikî Terimlderi. Intertnational Periodical fort he Languages, Literature and History of Turkish or Turkic 3/2: 191; Banu Mahir. Personal communication; see also Atıl, E. Süleymanname. The Illustrated History of Süleyman the Magnificient.

Court and City

Sources depicting Turkish long-necked lutes (*sazs*) are mainly to be found in urban iconography. Rural sources are virtually absent. A small three-stringed *saz* appears on one of the miniature paintings of the *Surnâme-i Hümayun* (1582), illustrating the circumcision festivities of Sultan Murad III's son Şehzade Mehmed. Several decades later, another Ottoman miniature painting from the *Ahmed I Album* (c. 1610), made on request of Sultan Ahmed I (r. 1603-1617), shows a female musician playing a three-stringed *saz* (c. 1610).

A genre of miniature paintings depicting a variety of musical instruments among which the *saz* are the by Metin And termed 'bazaar paintings'. Bazaar paintings, flourishing in Istanbul since the 17th century, emerged during the reign of the music loving Sultan Mehmed IV (r. 1648-1687), a period which saw an increase in music instruction of concubines (*câriyeler*). Bazaar paintings were generally commissioned by European travellers as 'souvenirs' of their trips and later assembled into albums. An important subject of these bazaar paintings was music, musical instruments, and dance.[63] A bazaar miniature painting from the so-called *Berlin Album* (c. 1640-1660), shows a *câriye* playing an eight-stringed *saz*, and another one from *Costumes de la Cour et de la Ville de Constantinople* (c. 1680-1690) *câriyeler* playing various instruments among which a five-stringed *saz*.[64]

Contrary to Ottoman miniature paintings, Safavid miniatures show a variety of long-necked lutes which. Since the Turkish lute tradition was strongly influenced by the Persian lute tradition, they give an impression of how the urban Turkish long-necked lutes may have looked like. The large variety of Turkish long-necked lutes in rural areas remain shrouded in history well into the 20th century.

The most important source for Turkish long-necked lutes is the *Seyâhatnâme* (1896) of Evliyâ Çelebi.[65] Born in a family with close ties to the Ottoman court, he became a 'royal entertainer and 'boon companion' (an intimate or drinking companion) of Sultan Murad IV (r. 1623-1640) having attracted his attention while performing Quran recitations in the Aya Sofia. He started to travel in 1640 and died in Cairo around 1684.[66] In the *Seyâhatnâme*, which is one of the most complete historical documents about Turkish musical instruments, all sorts of technical aspects are discussed, such as the shape of the bowl, the connection between bowl and neck, the material from which the soundboard was made (skin or wood), the material of the strings (silk, gut or brass), the arrangement of strings (single, two or three courses), the tuning, and the presence or absence of a bourdon and sympathetic strings, and possible 'inventors'. Evliyâ described various folk long-necked lutes, such as the *çöğür*, *çeşde*, *karadüzen*, *yonkar*, *yeltme*,

---

[63] Musician Concubines as seen by Turkish Bazaar Painters, in M. And Ottoman Figurative Arts 2: Bazaar Paintings: 103-114.

[64] Pekin, E. Theory, Instruments and Music, in İnalcık, H, and G. Renda. Ottoman Civilization 2: 1019-1022; Atasoy, N. Surname-I Hümayun. An Imperial Celebration; And, M (Geğirmenci, T. and M. Sabri Koz, eds). Ottoman Figurative Arts 2: Bazaar Painters: 15-16, 104-106, 148-149; Kahraman-Yücel Dağlı, A. Günümüz :Türkçesiyle Evliya Çelebi Seyahatnâmesi Istanbul: 637-642.

[65] The manuscript of the Seyâhatnâme was brought to Istanbul in 1742. The complete Turkish text appeared between 1896 and 1938.

[66] See for further reading Dankoff, R. and S. Kim. An Ottoman Traveller. Selections from the Book of Travels of Evliya Çelebi.

Figure 15. Musician playing a three-stringed *saz*. *Surnâme-i Hümayun*, 1582 (left). Woman playing a three-stringed *saz*. *Album Ahmed I, c.* 1610 (right).
© Topkapı Sarayı Müzesi, Istanbul. *Surnâme-i Hümayun*. H. 1344, 403b.
© Topkapı Sarayı Müzesi, Istanbul. *Album Ahmed I.* B. 408, 12A.

Figure 16. *Çâriye* playing an eight-stringed *saz* of which the neck ends in an artfully carved knob. *Berlin Album, c.* 1640-1660 (left). *Çâriyeler* playing a *kemânçe*, five-stringed *saz* (*çöğür*), and a *daire. Costumes de la Cour et de la Ville de Constantinople, c.* 1680-1690 (right).
© Staatlichen Museen Kunstbibliothek, Berlin. *Berlin Album.* K. 19774.
© Bibliothèque National de France, Paris.

tanbûra, tel tanbuûrası, sünder, şeşde, and şarkı. Unfortunately, only a few miniature paintings from the 17th century illustrate Evliyâ's extensive descriptions.[67]

We also know from the *Seyâhatnâme* that lutes occurred at the Ottoman court and in the Turkish cities and that these instruments were considerably better in quality than the simple ones used in the countryside. The popularity of the instrument in court circles indicate that not only the construction was raised to a higher level, but also that new and larger lute types evolved. According to Evliyâ, royal and learned persons played a role in the modification of existing lutes and in the 'invention' of new types. According to him, the five-string *çöğür* was invented by Yakûb (*d.* 1435), the bey of Germiyân (an area south-east of Kütahya) and the three-string *yonkar* by Şems Çelebi, a son of the 15th-century Ottoman poet Hamdi Çelebi (*d.* 1509).[68]

Our knowledge of the musical instruments at the Ottoman court in the 17th century is not only due to the *Seyâhatnâme*, but also to the payrolls of the court containing all kinds of information about numbers of players and their instruments, including long-necked lute players. Another source for the 17th century *sazs* is the *Saray-i Enderûn, cise Penetrale del Seraglio* (1665) by Wojciech Bobowski (1610–1675), a Polish prisoner of war, who stayed many years at the court of Sultan Murad IV under his Islamic name Ali Ufkî Bey.

The folk long-necked lutes mentioned by Bobowski in the *Saray-i Enderûn*, such as the *tchaganah* (*çagana*), *thchigour* (*çöğür*), *tanbourah* (*tanbura*), *teltanbourasi* (*teltanburası*), and *tscheschteh* (*çeşte*), were instruments used to accompany popular songs (*türküs*).[69] The *türküs* were introduced to the Ottoman court by court poets during the 17th century and it became fashionable to perform these songs among courtiers to the accompaniment of one of the long-necked lutes. One of these long-necked lutes (*tanbûra?*) was depicted on a miniature painting showing Sultan Murad IV surrounded by courtiers and servants in a courtyard of the Topkapı Sarayı (*c.* 1650). Long-necked lutes were also popular among the common people to accompany the popular *türküs* during indoor as well as outdoor festivities.[70]

Miniature paintings from the 17th century show that Turkish long-necked lutes, such as the Ottoman *tanbûr, şeştar, çöğür, tambura*, and *bozuk*, were mainly played by women at the Ottoman court.[71] The *çöğür* was, besides various other instruments such as the *kemânçe*, the *ney, mıskal*, and the *kanun*, one of the instruments instructed to talented women (*câriyeler*) of the *harem-i hümayun* (the imperial harem). A document from the Topkapı Sarayı Arşivi mentions a *çöğür* teacher Osman Ağa who instructed women not only in the *harem-i hümayun* but also at his home for which he received a monthly payment.[72]

---

[67] Feldman, W. Music of the Ottoman Court. Makam, Composition and the Early Ottoman Instrumental Reperoire: 169; Evliyâ Çelebi 2003. Günümüz Türkçesiyle Evliyâ Çelebi Seyahatnâmesi: Istanbul (Cilt 1). Kahraman, S.A. and Y. Dağlı (eds): 640-642.

[68] Kahraman-Yücel Dağlı, A. Günümüz :Türkçesiyle Evliya Çelebi Seyahatnâmesi Istanbul: 640-641.

[69] Feldman, W. Music of the Ottoman Court. Makam, Composition and the Early Ottoman Instrumental Reperoire: 169.

[70] Martin, R. Sarây-ı Enderûn. Albert Bobowski (Ali Ufki). Turkish Music Quarterly 3/4: 2; Feldman, W. Music of the Ottoman Court. Makam, Composition and the Early Ottoman Instrumental Repertoire: 169-173; See also Köprülü, F. (ed.). Türk sâz şairleri II: Antoloji, XVI-XVIII asırlar.

[71] Eroğlu, S. Frauen und das Spiel der Bağlama, in Çiftçi, N. and M. Greve (eds). Die Bağlama in der Türkei und Europa. Erstes Bağlama-Symposium in Deutschland. Berlin, 14-15 September 2013: 144.

[72] Uzunçarşılı, I.H. Osmanlılar Zamanında Saraylarda Musiki Hayatı: 87.

Figure 17. Sultan Murad IV surrounded by courtiers and servants in a courtyard of the Topkapı Sarayı. On the foreground a musician is playing a *saz* (*tanbura?*), one of the Turkish long-necked lutes used to accompany the popular *türküs*.
© Topkapı Sarayı Müzesi, Istanbul. H. 1248.

A miniature painting from the *Cigogna Album*, made for the Venetian Embassy in Istanbul and now preserved in the Museo Correr in Venice, shows Sultan Mehmed IV entering the harem with his son where he is welcomed by three female musicians, two of them playing a *saz*.[73] A women playing a *saz* (*çöğür?*) is also depicted on a miniature commissioned by Madame de Girardin, the wife of the French ambassador in Istanbul, and representing a reception organized by the Valide Sultan, the mother of the ruling sultan (2nd half 17th century).

Iconographical sources from the 17th and 18th centuries show long-necked lutes with a large number of frets to expand the tonal range and doubled or tripled strings played with a small or oval-shaped plectrum to obtain a stronger and fuller sound, Urban *saz*-culture was influenced by Ottoman classical music, including the *makam* tradition and the Ottoman *tanbûr*. An illustration of this influence is the depiction of a *tanbûr* (*bozuk?*) in the *Tefhîmü'l Makamat fî Tevlîd-in Neğamât* (The concept of the *makams* in the making of melodies, mid-18th century) by Kemânî Hızır Ağa (*d.* 1760?), a composer and musician at the court of Sultan Mahmûd I

---

[73] Sabri Koz, M. Preface: Ottoman Bazaar Painters, in M. And. Bazaar Painters: Ottoman Figurative Arts: 2: 17-20.

Figure 18. Women dancing and making music in front of the Valide Sultan, one of them playing a *çöğür*. The other instruments, from left to right, a *mıskal*, *def*, *ney*, and *kemânçe*. *Feste doneé à la Sultane Validée dans le Serail*, c. 1689.
© Le Département des Estampes de la Photographie, Paris. *Feste doneé à la Sultane Validée dans le Serail en présence de Me. Girardin Ambassadrice de France qui la fit preindre sur la liece et l'apporté à Paris. Elle est morte Comee. De Canillac.*

(*r.* 1730-1754). Striking are the large number of frets extending on the soundboard and the six strings arranged in courses. The composite soundboard and straight neck, the end of which has been artfully cut, are clearly visible. The inlay refers to an instrument from the Ottoman court or Ottoman elite. Another illustration is an amazing miniature painting by Abdullah Bûharî (1739) depicting a court woman playing a six-stringed *saz* with a plectrum.[74]

The Saz in the Work of European Artists and Travellers

Paintings, engravings, and drawings by European artists, as well as journals from European travellers who visited the Orient, are an important source of information for Turkish long-necked lutes. They reveal how long-necked lutes were not only popular among the Ottoman elite, but also among the common people and the Ottoman army to accompany popular *türküs* (folk songs).

---

[74] Feldman, W. *Music of the Ottoman Court. Makam, Composition and the Early Ottoman Instrumental Repertoire*: 171-173.

Figure 19. *Saz* with 33-34 frets played with a long plectrum like the Ottoman
tanbûr, detail of an image from a musical treaty of Kemânî Hızır Ağa (left). Court
woman playing a six-stringed *saz* (right).
© Kemânî Hızır Ağa *Tefhîmü'l Makamat fî Tevlîd-in Neğamât*.
© Istanbul Üniversitesi Kütüphanesi. *Abdullah-i Buhârî Albümü*. Ktp.,
TY, nr. 9364.

We owe images of long-necked lutes, among others, to the French painter Jean-Baptiste
Vanmour (1671-1737), who lived from 1699 until his death in Istanbul where he is buried in the
Jesuit church at Galata. Vanmour arrived in Istanbul on invitation of Marquis Charles de Ferriol
(1652-1722), the ambassador of Louis XIV (r. 1643-1715) to the Ottoman Empire from 1699 to
1709. He also worked for Cornelis Calkoen (1696-1764), the ambassador of the Dutch Republic
in Istanbul from 1725 to 1743.

Sultan Ahmed III admired the work of Vanmour and had his portrait made several times.
On *The Hunting Party of Sultan Ahmed III*, a musician is playing a small Turkish *saz* among the
dancing people in front of the sultan. Vanmour, who had a studio in Pera, painted in the style
of Jean-Antoine Watteau (1684-1721), whose paintings in Rococo style showed idyllic images of

Figure 20. People dancing and making music, one of them playing a small *saz*. On the background the Bosporus is visible. *The Hunting Party of Sultan Ahmed III* by Jean-Baptiste Vanmour.
© Christie's auction of Old Master Paintings, June 2004, catalogue: 77.

aristocratic life with elegantly dressed people in an outdoor setting known as 'fêtes galantes', such as *Partying Turkish courtiers* on which a musician is depicted playing a çöğür.[75]

Vanmour lived in Istanbul during one of the most fruitful periods of the arts in the Ottoman Empire, the *Lâle Devri* (1718-1730), named after the annual festivities to celebrate the blossoming of the tulip in the famous tulip gardens on the shores of the Bosporus. Under Sultan Ahmed III and his Grand Vizier Nevşehirli Damad Ibrahim Paşa (1666-1730) the Empire increasingly opened to the West. On the banks of the Bosporus and Golden Horn palaces and pavilions were erected with gardens in the French style for the urban elite and royal family. In those imperial gardens court musicians for the first time got in contact with the âşıks (folk poet-musicians) performing to the accompaniment of a *saz*.[76] They were also depicted by Levnî in the *Surnâme-i Vehbî* (Festival Book of Vehbî), one of the most comprehensive visual accounts of the *Lâle Devri* (Tulip Era, 1718-1730), which illustrated the circumcision rituals of four sons of Sultan Ahmed III in 1720.

Marquis Charles de Ferriol commissioned Vanmour to paint courtiers and people of Istanbul. On *Lady Mary Wortley Montagu with her son, Edward Wortley Montagu, and attendants*, Vanmour

---

[75] Davies, P.J.E. *et al.* Janson's History of Art: The Western Tradition: 763. Sint Nicolaas, E., D. Bull and G. Renda. De Ambassadeur, de Sultan en de Kunstenaar. Op audiëntie in Istanbul. Amsterdam: Rijksmuseum Dossiers.
[76] Shiloah, A. Music in the World of Islam. A Socio-Cultural Study: 92. See also: Köprülü, F. (ed.). Türk sâz şairleri II: Antoloji, XVI-XVIII. Köprülü, F. Türk Saz şairleri (19. Yüzyil Saz Şairleri).

Figure 21. Leisure scene in the Kâğıthane Park, near the Golden Horn, with on the background the
Sa'dâbâd palace, the summer palace of Sultan Ahmed III built in 1722. Engraving by l'Epinasse from the
Tableau Général de l'Empire Othoman. (1788-1824) of Ignace Mouradjea d'Ohsson (1740-1807). In the corner
sitting on a large carpet, men are smoking a *çubuk* while being entertained by musicians playing *sazs*
and a *ney*.
© Ignace Mouradjea d'Ohsson. *Tableau Général de l'Empire Othoman, divisé en deux parties, dont l'une
comprend la Législation Mahométane; l'autre l'Histoire de l'Empire Othomane.*

depicted the five-stringed *çöğür*, one of the larger long-necked lutes mentioned by Evliyâ
Çelebi and Wojciech Bobowski. The same instrument also appears on his *Fille Turque jouant du
Tchegour*, an engraving from the *Recueil de cent estampes*. After his return to France, Marquis
de Ferriol ordered to make gravures after these paintings and publish them in *Recueil de cent
estampes représentant différentes nations du Levant, gravées sur les tableaux peints d'après nature en
1707 & 1708 par les ordres de M. de Ferriol* (1714). Another painting of a long-necked lute by Vanmour
appeared as engraving in the *Recueil de cent estampes, Grec des Isles de L'Archipel joüant du Taboura.*
The *Recueil de cent estampes* was very successful and published in at least five languages across
Europe. It was used by various painters, designers, and porcelain makers as a primary source
for costumes, personages, and musical instruments of the Ottoman world.[77]

The *çöğür* was also depicted on an engraving in *Gabinetto Armonico* (1723) by Filip Bonanni
(1658-1723) with the caption *Calascione Turchesco*, being a copy of the instrument on *Fille Turque
jouant du Tchegour* from the *Recueil de cent estampes*. The *çöğür* was furthermore copied together
with a *kanun*, a copy of the instrument of *Fille du Turque jouant du Canon* from the *Recueil de
cent estampes*, a painting of an imaginary Ottoman interior by the Venetian painter Giovanni
Antonio Guardi (1699-1760).[78]

---

[77] Williams, H. Turquerie. An Eighteenth-Century European Fantasy: 49.
[78] See Sint Nicolaas, E., D. Bull and G. Renda. De Ambassadeur, de Sultan en de Kunstenaar. Op audiëntie in Istanbul.
Amsterdam, Rijksmuseum Dossiers.

Figure 22. Engraving *Fille Turque jouant du Tchegour* (left) and *Grec des Isles de l'Archipel jouant du Taboura* (right). *Recueil de cent estampes* commissioned by Marquis Charles de Ferriol after paintings by Jean-Baptiste Vanmour.
© M. de Ferriol. *Recueil de cent estampes représentant différentes nations du Levant, gravées sur les tableaux peints d'après nature en 1707 & 1708 par les ordres de M. de Ferriol.*

The *saz* was not only the instrument of professional poet-musicians, but also of the soldiers of the Ottoman army who were present everywhere in the Ottoman Empire. The most colourful of these were undoubtedly the so-called *bachi bazouks*, known for their roughness and cruelty. The French painter Jean-Léon Gérôme (1824-1904), who travelled through Turkey, Egypt, and North Africa, painted them several times. On *Bachi-Bouzouk chantant* (1868), Gérôme depicted a soldier accompanying himself on a small *saz*. The same instrument is also depicted on another painting by him, *Joueur de guitare. Chanteur grec* (1893).

In the 18th century, Europeans in Istanbul and the elites in Europe became eager to be depicted in Ottoman dress against the background of an imaginary oriental interior, a new vogue named 'turquerie'. It expressed the European vision of the Ottoman world visualized in a variety of art forms.[79] The Swiss painter Jean-Etienne Liotard (1702-1789), who called himself 'Le peintre turc', portrayed many members of the elite in this way. After having stayed Liotard at many prominent royal courts in Europe, he arrived in Istanbul in 1738, just after the death of Jean-Baptiste Vanmour. Liotard stayed in Istanbul for four more years, maybe to fill the gap on the

---

[79] See for further reading Williams, H. Turquerie. An Eighteenth-Century European Fantasy: 7.

Figure 23. *Bachi bouzouk* (Turkish *başıbozuk*) playing a small *saz, Bachi-Bouzouk chantant* (1868) by Jean-Léon Gérôme.
© Courtesy The Walters Art Museum, Baltimore. *Bachi-Bouzouk chantant*. Inv. nr. 37.883.

artistic market, left by Vanmour. On *M. Levett et Mlle. Glavani en costume turc* of 1740, Liotard depicted in Hélène Glavani, the daughter of the former French consul in the Crimea between 1723 and 1734, 'playing' an Ottoman *tanbûr*. Besides her on the Ottoman *divan* stands a six-stringed *saz* with inlay of mother-of-pearl. The composited soundboard and number of strings are clearly visible.

The first *kahvehanes* (coffee houses) appeared in the streets of Istanbul in the 2nd half of the 16th century. Already in an early stage these *kahvehanes* became places where travelling âşıks performed their epics and poetry to the accompaniment of a *saz*. These *kahvehanes* became particularly popular in the 17th century with the Janissaries, the sultan's elite troops. Listening to an *aşık* became almost as important as - perhaps even more important than - drinking coffee. These so-called âşık-*kahvehanes* played an important role in the social and cultural life of Istanbul during the 18th and early 19th century.

Âşıks were depicted several times, among others in *Intérieur d'un café à Boyh Deré près de Constantinople* and *Café de Galata á Constantinople* (1878-1882) by the French Orientalist painter Théodore Frère (1814-1888), and in *Coffee house by the Ortaköy mosque in Constantinople* (1864) by the Russian-Armenian painter Ivan Konstanovitch Aivazovsky (1817-1900). Both stayed in Istanbul and depicted an urban âşık playing a large *saz* (*divan sazı*?). On both paintings, the number of tuning pegs indicate strings arranged in courses and while the frets continuing on the soundboard are clearly visible, a feature which still appears on the large Turkish long-necked lutes until the 2nd half of the last century.

Figure 24. *M. Levett et Mlle. Glavani en costume turc* by Jean-Étienne Liotard, 1740.
Francis Levett, an English merchant and collector of the work of Liotard, is dressed
as an Ottoman gentleman wearing a fur-trimmed robe and turban smoking a
Turkish *çubuk*. Hélène Glavani wears a traditional Tartar costume and 'plays' an
eight-stringed Ottoman *tanbûr* with a long tortoise shell plectrum. Besides her on
the Ottoman divan stands a beautifully ornamented six-stringed *saz*.
© Author, *M. Levett et Mlle. Glavani en costume turc*. Musée du Louvre, Paris. AKG
230609.

Led by various sultans, the government implemented a reform policy in Istanbul between 1839 and 1876, a period called 'Tanzimat' in Ottoman historiography (derived from *Tanzimat-i hayriye*, or 'Happy Reorganization'). The resistance of the Janissaries to this reform policy led in 1826 to their termination by Sultan Mahmûd II (*r.* 1808-1839). Partly as a result of this, the *âşık* coffeehouses, where the *saz* occupied such an important place, disappeared. Cafe chantant appeared with other forms of entertainment, resulting in the replacement of the *saz* by other instruments.

The popular Turkish shadow play *Karagöz* (Turkish for Black Eyes or Gypsy),[80] performing various stories including political and social satire, was also performed in the coffee houses throughout mainly from the 17th to the 19th century. The introduction of Western culture in the 19th century, later followed by the advent of cinema, radio, and television, led to a loss in popularity of *Karagöz*. One of the characters of this shadow play is *âşık* Hasan performing to the accompaniment of a *saz*. In one of the *Karagöz* scenarios, *Karagöz* takes part in an *âşık* poetry

---

[80] Southeast Asia is considered to be the origin of the Turkish shadow theatre. According to another opinion Sultan Selim I brought shadow theatre artists to Turkey after he conquered Egypt in 1517.

Figure 25. Urban âşık playing a *divan sazı* in a *kahvehane* at Büyükdere, *Intérieur d'un café à Boyh Deré près de Constantinople* by Théodore Frère, 1878-1882. Büyükdere (Turkish for 'The Big Valley'), once one of the fishing villages located along the European shore of the Bosporus, was a popular destination for daytrips.
© Musée du Quai Branly, Paris. *Intérieur d'un café à Boyh Deré près de Constantinople*.

contest, simulating playing a *saz* with a broom, winning the first prize, "not by his talent in improvising poems on given rhymes and themes, but by his rudeness and violence".[81]

The Saz in Anatolian Folk Music

The separation between urban and rural culture increased after the establishment of the Ottoman Empire. This separation which was mirrored by the difference between the more sophisticated urban *sazs* and the simple rural ones. In urban centres of strong artistic creativity, musical instruments practices flourished, whereas in the static rural areas, musical instruments remained practically unaltered for centuries. This situation only changed after the rise of the Republic of Turkey in 1923.

Sources to reconstruct the folk musical folk traditions and instruments of Anatolia are almost absent. The lack of urban centres and the destruction of libraries and archives during the wars of the 19th and 20th centuries are the main reason. What we do know is that long-necked lutes were very popular among the Turks of Anatolia and that they were played in the folk musical traditions, during the religious ceremonies of the Bektaşî and Alevî, by the *ozans* and *âşıks*, and were also popular among the soldiers of the Seljuk and Ottoman army.

---

[81] And, M. Karagöz. Turkish Shadow Theatre: 168, 197 (see also for further reading).

Figure 26. Characters of the Turkish shadow play *Karagöz*, in the centre *Âşık* Hasan and on the right a
Laz, being a member of a group inhabiting the coastal regions of the Black Sea, playing a *kemençe* (left).
Karagöz simulating with a broom the playing of a *saz* (right).
© Museum of Turkish and Islamic Art, Istanbul.
© Yapı Kredi Yayınları, Istanbul. And, M. *Karagöz. Turkish Shadow Theatre*: 168.

The Saz in the Âşık, Alevî, and Bektaşî Tradition

Poet-musicians (*ozans*) have been travelling around in Central Asia since the 9th and 10th
century performing epics, religious songs, and autobiographical songs to the accompaniment
of the *kopuz*. The *ozans* sang the glory of the chiefs of the nomadic tribes which they visited and
the rulers and princes by whom they were employed.[82]

The disappearance of the *ozan* in the 15th-century probably resulted from the spread of Islam
and the rise of a culture oriented towards Islamic values and Arabic language and literature.
Moreover, Sûfîsm initiated a growing interest in *tanbûrs*, which became the lute of the poet-
musicians, replacing the *kopuz*. In Anatolia, the Turks adopted the name *âşık* in the 15th
century, derived from the Arabic *ašıq*, meaning lover, in a new religious context acquiring the
meaning of an interpreter of the love for Allah, Ali, or some saint. The name ozan became
associated with the pre-Islamic period. The *âşıks*, who were also called *saz* şairleris ('poets with
a *saz*'), wandered with their *saz* from *tekke* to *tekke*, coffee house to coffee house, city to city, and
village to village. They were inspired by the Islamic tradition, the legends of famous saints, the
old Persian epics, or contemporary subjects and events.[83]

Nowadays, *âşıks* and their audience prefer secular themes. Religious issues gradually lost their
importance in song contest, although this may change again under the current conservative
climate. Song contests have become a commercial activity without a winner or loser in
coffeehouses. The major goal of *âşıks* is to entertain the audience. Contemporary *âşıks*, who
are skilled *bağlama* players say that the long-necked lute is a source of inspiration. Moreover

---

[82] During, J., R. Sultanova and A. Djumaev 2000. Zentralasien: 2363; see poet-musician tradition in Zeeuw, J. de, Tanbûr
Long-Necked Lutes along the Silk Road and beyond; see furthermore Reinhard, U. and T. de Oliveira Pinto. Sänger und
Poeten mit der Laute. Türkische Âşık und Ozan: 12-78.
[83] Köprülü, F.M. Early Mystics in Turkish Literature: 174.

it is a good way to gain time during a performance helps them 'to hide and correct errors'. As a matter of fact, without a *bağlama* most *âşık*s would be unable to improvise poetry during a song contest.[84]

In contemporary Turkey, the reputation and influence of *âşık*s are changing due to the influence of a growing urbanization, modern media, and shifting interests towards Western music, although there are still many *âşık*s of a younger generation in Anatolia. Nevertheless, the death of the famous and charismatic *âşık*s Murat Çobanoğlu (1940-2005) and Şeref Taşlıova (1938-2014), both from Kars, was a blow to the traditional *aşık* tradition.[85]

Less known in Turkey are the female *âşık*s. Like female musicians in Central Asia they experience a conflict between their position as women in a society that obstructs their artistic aspirations and being a *âşık*. In their poetry, they criticize their social position as is the case in the moving 'Sarıcakız' (Turkish for a blonde-haired girl) by *âşık* Ilkin Manya:[86]

Gün oldu dövüldük yere post olduk	Sometimes we were beaten and we were made into a doormat
Susturdular heykel olduk bust olduk	Sometimes we were silenced such as statue such as bust
Acıyla yaşadık dertle dost olduk	We have lived with hurt and we became friends with sorrow
Yutkunup ümükte düglemedik mi	We gulped down our sorrows, didn't we
At kaderi it kaderi	Destiny of horse destiny of dog
Ille de avrat kaderi	Necessarily destiny of wife

Like the *âşık*s Mahsuni Şerif and Feyzullah Çınar in the past, female *âşık*s run the risk of imprisonment. *Âşık* Şahturna Ağdaşan (1950), who discusses political, social, and religious issues in her poetry was arrested several times. She was forced to flee to Germany in 1978. She was stripped of her citizenship – but regained it in 1992. She stayed in Berlin where she continues to work and perform, occasionally still performing in Turkey as well.[87]

The two foremost brotherhoods are the Bektaşî and the Alevî.[88] The Alevî owe their name to Ali bn-Abi Talîb (*c.* 600-661), cousin and son-in-law of the Prophet and the fourth caliph or successor to the Prophet and the first Shi'ite imam. The Bektaşî order is named after the mystic Hacı Bektaş Veli (1247-1337) who arrived in Anatolia from Khurâsân.

Unlike the orthodox Sunnis, who are generally suspicious of music, the Shi'ite Bektaşî and Alevî considered music and dance as means for man to come to spiritual enlightenment and thus unite with God. Music, poetry, singing and ritual dance are the essence of their religious

---

[84] Erdener, Y. 2001. Turkish Song Duel, in V. Danielson, S. Marcus and D. Reynolds (eds) The Garland Encyclopedia of World Music. The Middle East Volume 6: 801-809.

[85] Reinhard, U. and V. Reinhard. Song Creators in Eastern Turkey (CD-Booklet): 35 and registration 7. See for a short biography of Murat Çobanoğlu and Şeref Taşlıova: 14-19.

[86] Çinar, S. Yirminci Yüzyılın Ikinici Yasında Türkiye'de Âşıklar; Çinar, S. Giriş (Introduction). Kadın Âşıklar (CD-Booklet): 64.

[87] Çinar, S. Giriş (Introduction). Kadın Âşıklar (CD-Booklet): 72-73.

[88] See Mélikoff, I. Bektashi/Kızılbaş: Historical Bipartition and Its Consequences. In: Alevi Identity: 1-7; Köprülü, M.F. A Bektashî tradition, in M.F. Köprülü, Early Mystics in Turkish Literature: 268-269.

Figure 27. Şeref Taşliova and Murat Çobanoğlu 'duelling' in Cobanoğlu's Âşık café in Kars, north-eastern Turkey.
© Yapı Kredi Yayınları, Istanbul. Erdener, Y. *Kars'ta Çobanoğlu Kahvehanesi'nde Âşık Karşılaşmaları. Âşıklık Geleneğinin Şamanizm ve Sufizmle Olan Taihsel Bağları*: 251.

experience. During their religious gatherings (*âyîn-i cem*, ceremony of union), in which women are also be present, mystical songs such as the *nefes*, *ilahi*, and the *mersiye* were sung and accompanied on the *bağlama*.[89] Singing the *nefes* or *deyiş* songs arouses ecstasy among the participants of the *âyîn-i cem* and men and women dance together the *sema* accompanied by one or more *bağlamas*.[90] The Alevî also call the *bağlama* the *telli Kur'an* (the 'stringed *Qur'an*'). The bowl symbolizes Alî (Alî ibn Abî Tâlib (600-661), cousin and son-in-law of the Prophet and the fourth of the 'rightly guided' caliphs (*al-râshidûn*), and the neck refers to his two-bladed sword *Zülfikâr*.[91]

The Diffusion of the Saz

Turkish long-necked lutes travelled throughout the Ottoman Empire to south-eastern Europe in the 14th and 15th centuries. Local variants emerged such as the four-stringed *bouzoúki* and *baghlamádhes*, and the *tamburas* (*tambouras*) on the Balkan.[92]

---

[89] Bektaşi Nefesleri 3. The Bektashi Breathes 3 (CD-Booklet): 8.
[90] Cler, J. and J. During. Turkey. The Djem Alevi Ceremony (CD); Cler, J. The Ceremony of the Bektashi Djem (CD).
[91] See Mélikoff, I. Bektaşî / Kızılbaş: Historical Bipartition and Its Consequences and Cler, J. and J. During. The Djem Alevi Ceremony (CD-Booklet); Cler, J. Turquie. Cérémonie de Djem Bektashi. La tradition d'Abdal Musa (CD-Booklet): 12-19.
[92] Bezić, J., M. Gavazzi , M. Jakelić M. and P. Mihanović. Tradicijska Narodna Glazbala Jugoslavije (Traditional Folk Musical Instruments of Jugoslavia): 41; Rene Grémaux. Personal communication; See for further reading Zeeuw, J. de. Chapter 6 Saz, in J. de Zeeuw, Tanbûr Long-Necked Lutes along the Silk Road and beyond:106-136.

Figure 28. Men and women performing a *sema* (religious dance) to the accompaniment of two *bağlamas*
during the Abdal Musa festival in Tekkeköy, near Antalya.
© Courtesy Ergun Çağatay (1937-2018), Istanbul.

Since the 16th century, during the conquest of the Middles East, Turkish long-necked lutes also travelled to Syria, Lebanon, Iraq, and Egypt. In northern Syria and Lebanon, long-necked lutes are in general played by non-Arabs to accompany love songs and epic tales, as solo instrument or accompanied by a rhythmic instrument at festivals and important life cycle events. In northern Iraq, long-necked lutes (*saz* and *tanbûr*) are mainly played by Turkmens and Kurds to accompany songs. In Egypt, the long-necked (*tanbûrs*), discussed by Guillaume-André Villoteau (1759-1839), were generally played by non-Arabs. They now seem to have fallen into oblivion.[93]

Turkish long-necked lutes probably also travelled with the Ottoman army to southern Italy during the occupation of Otranto in 1480-1481. Around 1484 the composer and musical theorist Johannes Tinctoris (*c.* 1435-1511) described in his *De inventione et usu musice* (The Invention and Use of Music) a Turkish '*tambûrâ*' in southern Italy as follows: 'shaped like a great spoon, has three strings tuned to an octave, a 5th, and a 4th, struck to be sounded by the fingers or a quill'. Once introduced, the *tambûrâ* probably developed into the *colascione* (*colachon* or *callichone*). The *colascione* was a popular instrument in Italy in from the 15th to the 17th century and was

---

[93] Hassan, S.Q. Syria: 855; Hassan, S.Q. The Long Necked Lute in Iraq: 1-2, 8; See for further reading Zeeuw, J. de. Chapter 6 Saz, in J. de Zeeuw, Tanbûr Long-Necked Lutes along the Silk Road and beyond:37-38, 52-55, 106-136.

Figure 29. *Tambourá* resting on a divan. *Dames de L'Ile de Tines*, engraving from *Voyage pittoresque de la Grèce*, 1782 (left). Macedonian *tamboura* (right).
© Marie-Gabriel-Florent-Auguste Comte de Choiseul-Gouffier. *Voyage pittoresque de la Grèce*.
© Courtesy Atlas of Plucked Instruments.

depicted many times on engravings and paintings. Nowadays, the *colascione* is a uncommon instrument.[94]

The Greek *rebétika* as we know it today appeared in the musical cafés, jail, and hashish's *tekés* in the large cities such as Athens, Salonica, and especially Piraeus, after the influx of refugees from Asia Minor, especially Smyrna (nowadays Izmir) in 1924. The population exchange between Turkey and Greece in 1924 involved most of the native Muslims of Greece and nearly all the Orthodox Christian citizens of Turkey and. Among them were many professional musicians and their instruments among which various Turkish long-necked lutes. The small sized *baghlamádhes* were probably the most representative instruments of the early *rebétika* (or *rembetiko*). They were very popular among musicians as they were easy to transport or hidden under a coat.[95]

The Republic of Turkey

On October 29, 1923, the Republic of Turkey (Türkiye Cumhuriyeti) was proclaimed in Ankara with Mustafa Kemal Paşa (1881-1938), the later Atatürk ('Father of the Turks'), as its first president. This important historical event had a major impact on Ottoman classical music

---

[94] Tinctoris, J. The Complete Theoretical Works; Schossig, D. Der Colascione – eine Langhalslaute des 17./18. Jh.: 7, 16.
[95] Shields, Sarah. The Greek-Turkish Population Exchange: Internationally Administered Ethnic Cleansing. Middle East Report (267): 2-6; Anoyanakis, F. Greek Popular Musical Instruments: 210; Zeeuw, J. de. Tanbûr Long-Necked Lutes along the Silk Road and beyond: 117-121; see for further reading Holst, G. Road to Rembetika.

Figure 30. From large to small the *tanbour charqy, tanbour bouzourk, tanbour baghlama,* and *tanbour boulghâry.* Customized engraving *Description de l'Égypte ou recueil des observations et de recherches qui ont été faites en Egypte* (1823) of Guillaume-André Villoteau. (right). A mid-18th century ensemble in Aleppo consisting of a *daire, saz, ney, kemenche,* and a *naqqâra* (right).
© Villoteau, G-A. *Description de l'Égypte ou recueil des observations et de recherches qui ont été faites en Egypte. Des instrumens a cordes connus en Egypte.* Planches. Planche AA, Tome 2: E.M. Vol II. PL. AA.
© Russel, A. and P. Russel. *The Natural History of Aleppo:* Plate 4.

Figure 31. Drawing by Pietro Longhi (1701-1785) of a musician playing a three-stringed *colascione,* mid-18th century. Three-stringed *colascione* by Karl Kirchmeyr, Vienna, after a by Andrea Lignoli in 1600 built *colascione.*
© Copyrights unknown.
© Courtesy Karl Kirchmeyr, Vienna.

Figure 32. The fish market in the Greek port of Piraeus in 1937. On the left the in Piraeus born *saz* virtuoso Iovan Saouz (left). *Baghlamádhes* ranging from 40 to 50 cm (right).
© Courtesy Denise Harvey (Publisher), Greece. Holst, G. *Road to Rembetika*. Illustration page 28.
© Courtesy Melissa Publishing House, Athens. Anoyanakis, F. *Greek Popular Musical Instruments*: 95.

and the folk musical traditions of Anatolia, resulting in a modification and standardization of Turkish folk musical instruments. A variety of folk musical instruments, of which the *saz/bağlama* became a central instrument and a national symbol as well, are played in the various genres of the Turkish folk musical traditions, either as a solo instrument, as an accompanying instrument or in ensembles and orchestras, including the *zurna* (a double-reed oboe), the *mey* (shepherd's pipe, shawn), *kaval* (shepherd's flute), *çifte* (clarinet), *kemane* (fiddle), *kemenche* (fiddle), *davul* (big drum), *darbuka*, *zil* (metal castanets), *kaşık* (spoons), *dümbelek* (small drum), *cümbüş* (sort of banjo), *sipsi* (small shepherd's flute), and the *def* (tambourine).[96]

One of the main objectives of the new republic was to raise a national Turkish consciousness among the population and one of the means to achieve this goal was the formation of a national music culture (*milli musîkî*). The ideologist Mehmet Ziya Gökalp (1875-1925), whose ideas had a great influence on Atatürk, played an important role in this process. Gökalp believed that the Ottoman Empire had alienated the Turks from their Central Asian past and that there was a socio-cultural separation between the Ottoman elite on and the Turkish common people, which was, among other things, illustrated for example by the coexistence of two forms of music, Ottoman classical music and Anatolian folk music.[97]

In order to end to this separation, Turkish society and culture had to focus on their Central Asian past and on Europe in the context of modernization and progress. Regarding Turkish music, Gökalp thought that only one musical tradition should remain, namely Turkish folk music, enriched with elements of European music. Given its elite character and being a typical exponent of decadent Ottoman court life, Ottoman classical music was banned from modern Turkish culture.

---

[96] Picken, L. Folk Musical Instruments of Turkey: 239-240.
[97] Pirker, M. K. Atatürks reform und das Musikleben in der Türkei. Musicologica Austriaca 12: 33-39.

Establishing a theory of Turkish folk music (*halk müziği*) would contribute to the rise of a nation state and a national consciousness. Strikingly, musicologists trained in the tradition of urban Ottoman classical music, such as Veysel Arseven (1919-1977) and Halil Bedi Yönetken (1899-1968), played an important role in the development of a theory of folk music in imitation of Ottoman classical music and the Ottoman *tanbûr*. The establishment of a theory of folk music resulted in a modernization and standardization of Turkish folk music based on the definition and systematization of a body of modal structures, instrument tunings, and rhythms inseparable linked to the *saz*.[98]

The Saz and the Establishment of a National Musical Culture

In order to materialize the ideology, formulated by Ziya Gökalp, conservatories and research institutes were established in the 1930s, and Anatolian folk music was collected, recorded, and archived. The archive for Turkish folk music was initially housed in the Ankara State Conservatory, founded in 1936 with the help of Paul Hindemith (1895-1963). In 1967 this archive was transferred to the Turkish Radio and Television (TRT, Türkiye Radyo ve Televizyonu).

The TRT became the most important institute for the collection, registration, notation, and archiving of Turkish folk music. Research, collection, concert life and state media politics became even more closely intertwined and led to the creation of a Turkish national musical canon was created at the expense of the local and regional diversity of the Anatolian traditions of folk music. The TRT performed folk music in a more or less standardized way, modelled on Ottoman classical music, by soloists, choirs, and orchestras in which the *saz* played an important role.

To spread Turkish national music to the population, radio broadcasts took place since 1938 and concerts were organized in *halk evleri* (folk houses) and *halk odaları* (people's rooms). Since 1950, a large amount of folk music collected in the field has, moreover been printed and spread by various publishers. From the 1970s, this role was increasingly taken over by television. Radio and television thus played an important role in the propagation of the new national music and the formation of a Turkish national identity. The *saz* became the central instrument in music education at *dershanes* (private institutions).

The *âşıks* played an essential role in the distribution of Turkish folk music in Anatolia. One of the most key representatives of the *âşık* tradition of the last century was Âşık Veysel (1894-1973). Blind from the age of seven, Veysel was 'discovered' during an *âşık* festival in Sivas in 1931. He contributed greatly to the promotion and popularization of Turkish folk music and to the popularization of the *saz* through performances and recordings.

Radio, television, and education largely determine the identity of Turkish national music and the development of the musical taste of the general public. However, notwithstanding the increasing influence of the media (whether or not Western) , folk music in Turkey is still a

---

[98] Traditionally, folk music was transmitted entirely aurally and orally; See for discussion Okan Murat Öztürk, Die Befreiung der in Anatolien gespielten Bağlama-Familie in terminologischer, typologischer und tonräumlicher Hinsicht, in Çiftçi, N. and M. Greve (eds) Die Bağlama in der Türkei und Europa. Erstes Bağlama-Symposium in Deutschland. Berlin, 14-15 September 2013: 44, 37-62; Stokes, M. The Arabesk Debate. Music and Musicians in Modern Tuerkey: 51.

Figure 33. Âşık Veysel during an open air concert to school children in Karatepe
(south-eastern Anatolia) in 1961.
© Türkiye Cumhuriyeti Kültür Bakanlığı. Turan, M., G. Öz and O. Yılmaz. *Dostlar
Seni Unutmadı/The Friends Still Remember You*: 75.

living tradition playing an important role during social events such as birth, marriage, death, circumcision, seasonal festivals, and religious ceremonies.

When Turkish researchers began to approach Turkish folk music more scientifically, the folklore departments at Turkish universities were closed. Turkish folklore has since been covered by Turkish literature at schools and universities, which are under the control of the Turkish Ministry of Culture and Tourism (*Türkiye Cumhuriyeti Kültür ve Turizm Bakanlığı*). Scientific research became part of their political-ideological activities and an officially sanctioned image of Turkish folk music and the origin of the *saz*/ba*ğlama*.[99]

The establishment of a museum and research centre for Turkish folk music and folk musical instruments according to international standards and non-ideological approach of Turkish folk music are therefore of great importance. Laurence Picken (1909-2007) already argued

---

[99] See Conrad, J. The Political Face of Folklore. A Call for a Debate. The Journal of American Folklore 11; Papagu, D.W. The Folk, the State and the Prophets: Poetry, Music and Politics in a Turkish Province; Öztürk, O.M. Die Befreiung der in Anatolien gespielten Bağlama-Familie in terminologischer, typologischer und tonräumlicher Hinsicht, in Çiftçi, N. and M. Greve (eds) Die Bağlama in der Türkei und Europa. Erstes Bağlama-Symposium in Deutschland. Berlin, 14-15 September 2013: 44, 37-62.

in 1975 that a national catalogue of which the traditional instruments, located in various provincial museums and private collections, should be compiled. In May 2006, in anticipation of the establishment of a museum for Turkish music, the *Uluslararası Müzik Kongresi* took place in Istanbul. The establishment of an independent museum could play an important role in stimulating scientific research and publications, and in making collections and archives accessible. Unfortunately, such a museum has still to be established.

The Development of the Contemporary Bağlama

Due to the modern entertainment industry and the changing taste of the audience, musicians increasingly developed virtuoso playing techniques. This resulted in gradually higher demands on technical and artistic capacities of their instruments. The playing techniques grew still more sophisticated when in the late 1970s it became possible to study folk music at the state conservatories with the *bağlama* as basic instrument.

In the post-1960s, Turkish folk music underwent a major development under the influence of *bağlama* virtuosos such as Talip Özkan (1939-2010), Yavuz Top (1950), Nida Tüfekçi (1929-1993), Ali Ekber Çiçek (1935-2006), Neşet Ertaş (1938-2012), Arif Sağ (1945), Musa Eroğlu (1946), and Yilmaz İpek (1936). Virtuosity increased and new playing techniques evolved initiating the development of new *bağlama* types.

The *bağlama* underwent a number substantial structural changes. The smaller U and cone-shaped bowl without a sound hole and an arched and composed soundboard turned into a larger U and pear-shaped bowl with a sound hole under the rim of the bowl. These changes resulted in a more powerful volume and 'warmer' timbre compared to the silvery sounding timbre of the traditional *bağlama*.

In addition, on both the first and third and sometimes also second string course, one of the steel strings was replaced by an octave string (*bam teli*), a wounded steel string. The expansion of the number of frets resulted in further melodic refinement. The expansion of the number of frets and their tuning, a development in which Muzaffer Sarısözen (1899-1963) played an important role, already started in the 1940s. On a photograph from 1944 Sarısözen is depicted with a saz on which the frets, made of reed (*kamış perdesi*), extend on the soundboard. On a photograph of him from 1951 this is no longer the case. The frets are only positioned on the initially extended neck. In the same period, experiments were carried out with tempered frets.

The development of a virtuous way of playing required, however, a shorter neck. Moreover, the longer the neck, the higher the string tension and the higher the pressure on the soundboard. This problem was solved by changing the shape of the bowl from ovoid to pear-shaped, making it possible to extend the neck 'inwards'. In this way, the neck could be kept relatively short. In order to obtain a better distribution of the tension over the entire string length (mensur), the characteristic straight neck of the *bağlama* was replaced by a neck with an angled pegbox. According to Cafer Açın (1939-2012) it was the luthier Yusuf Atasoy from Ankara who introduced the angled pegbox around 1950.[100]

---

[100] Cafer Açın. Personal communication.

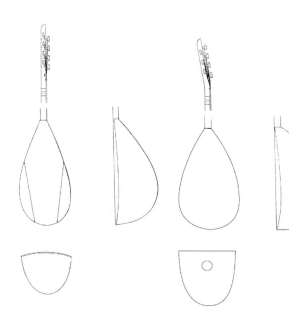

Figure 34. The smaller U and cone-shaped bowl without sound hole and a curved and composite soundboard and straight evolved into a larger U and pear-shaped bowl with a sound hole under the tailpiece and a flat one-piece soundboard and an angled pegbox.
© Cafer Açın / Author, Istanbul.

Around 1980 this process was largely completed, resulting in the *baǧlama* family consisting of the *cura*, long-necked *baǧlama* and short-necked *baǧlama*, *tambura*, *divan sazı*, and *meydan sazı*. The first *baǧlamas* with a shorter neck were already built in the 1960s, but this instrument did not really become popular until Arif Saǧ started to play a short-necked *baǧlama* type developed around 1980 by the luthier Kemal Eroǧlu, influencing a younger generation of *baǧlama* players. Many musicians, however, including Arif Saǧ himself, are of the opinion that the short-necked *baǧlama* is not a contemporary but a very old instrument.

In reality, the development of the short-necked *baǧlama* was probably the result of a change in the way the *baǧlama* was played. The traditional Turkish playing technique is based on the rapid movement of the left hand along the entire length of the neck. The so-called grip technique on string instruments such as guitar and violin is completely different. The left hand is held as much as possible in the same position when playing tones that are more than a quarter apart enabling the playing of chords and polyphony.

Around the 1960s some musicians began to explore the possibilities of this technique on the long-necked *baǧlama* tuned in *baǧlama düzeni*. The starting point was the question of how certain passages could be played efficiently, using all the possibilities of the instrument systematically. It soon became clear that some structural adjustments had to be made to the instrument itself. The problem was that the frets were too far apart to allow a quiet hand position. The use of shorter strings makes it possible to sufficiently reduce the distance between the successive frets. That is why the short-necked *baǧlama* (*kısa saplı baǧlama*) is ten to twelve centimetres shorter (one note) than the long-necked *baǧlama* (*uzun saplı baǧlama*).

The need for an instrument with a larger sound volume increased after the 1960s. Initially, ordinary microphones were used, but soon the installation of small amplification elements in the bridge or on the soundboard were installed. Besides the electrically amplified acoustic *baǧlama*, the *electrobaǧlama* (electric *baǧlama*) evolved. The modern *electrobaǧlama* has its

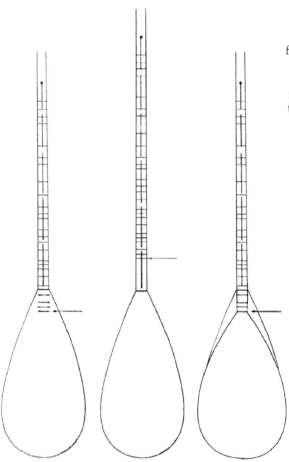

Figure 35. Expansion of the number of frets, using the soundboard and extending the neck. A more virtuoso playing technique, however, required a shorter neck that was made possible by changing the shape of the bowl from ovoid to pear-shaped, making it possible to extend the neck 'inwards'.
© Cafer Açın / Author, Istanbul.

own timbre and the playing style differs from the *bağlama* playing style The instrument is especially popular in the arabesque music played amongst others in the gazinos (casinos). In the meantime, *electrobağlamas* are also being built with a flat solid block of wood instead of a bowl-shaped resonator.[101]

Towards a New Generation of Bağlamas

After the 1980s, a new generation of *bağlamas* evolved with variants such as the *dört telli bağlama* (the four-course *bağlama*), the *perdesiz tanbura* (the fretless *tanbura*), the *electro bass bağlama* (the electric bass *bağlama*), the *semi-akustik bağlama* (the *semi-acoustic bağlama*) and the *Oğur sazı*, an instrument designed by Erkan Oğur, and its variants. Further experiments with the arrangement of the frets and strings, and their tunings as well as playing techniques are being conducted on these instruments.

---

[101] Stokes, M.H. The media and reform: the saz and elektrosaz in urban Turkish Folk Music. British Journal of Ethnomusicology 1: 89-102.

The *dört telli bağlama* can be considered as the continuation of a development that started with the short-necked *bağlama* (*kısa saplı bağlama*). To increase the vertical and harmonic possibilities, a fourth course was added. The length of the neck of the *dört telli bağlama* equals the neck of the short-necked *bağlama*, but its neck is wider while its bowl is larger. The *dört telli bağlama* can be played in the traditional Turkish horizontal position, the melody being played, or in a more vertical way the melody being played on all four string course in multiple tunings.

The *perdesiz tanbura* and *semi-akustik bağlama* played by Okan Murat Öztürk also belong to a new generation of *bağlamas*. The *perdesiz klassik gitar* from Erkan Oğur initiated the development of the *perdesiz tanbura*. The absence of frets enables glissandos, slides, and legatos creating a mystical timbre. The *perdesiz tanbura* lends itself perfectly to play *taksîms* and *açış* melodies, as well as *uzun havas*, mystical songs, and melancholic *türküs*.

The short-necked *acoustic bass bağlama*, also belongs to the new generation of *bağlamas* which evolved after the 1980s. The bowl of the *acoustic bass bağlama* is composed of ribs (*yapraklı*), the bowl of the *electric bass bağlama*, and fretless *electric bass bağlama* are carved-hollowed-out

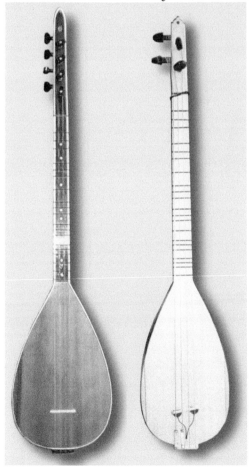

(*oyma*). The *bass bağlama* replaced the *divan sazı* as bass instrument.

Another example of how the *bağlama* inspires new forms is shown by the *Yaren sazı*, consisting of a *tanbura*, *bağlama*, and *cura*, played by Özay Gönlüm (1940-2000) and made by Cafer Açın in 1974 and the *divan sazı* made by the luthier Yavuz Gül (Divane, Izmir). The *Yaren sazı* initiated the creation of a number of variants such as the *Koşasaz*, a combination of a *saz* and a *cura*, and the *Aras bağlama*, a *tanbûra* and a short-neck *bağlama* of which the bowl is carved from a single block of wood. Searching for a more powerful sound volume than the *divan sazı*, Yavuz Gül developed the *divane* of which the neck equals the neck of the long-necked *bağlama* and the bowl resembles the bowl of the *'ûd* and its variants such as the *lavta*. The *divan* family consists of the *efe divane*, the *baba divane*, the *divane deli*, and the *bass divane*.

Inspired by the lute and the guitar, the luthier Süleyman developed a bracing system to support the soundboard and positions a rod in the neck to prevent collapsing of the soundboard and warping of the neck due to the string tension. He furthermore positions the neck in a rectangular instead of a V-shaped joint. These

Figure 36. *Dört telli bağlama* and *electric bas bağlama*.
© Author.

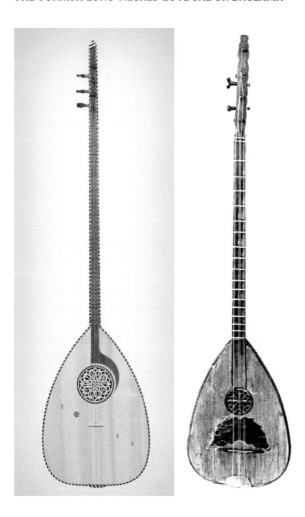

Figure 37. The *baba divane* of Yavuz Gül.
The similarities with a Greek *bouzoúki*
from around nineteen hundred are
striking.
© Courtesy Yavuz Gül, Izmir.
© Courtesy Denise Harvey (Publisher),
Greece. Holst, G. *Road to Rembetika*.
Illustration page 69.

changes enabled him to build on request of Kemal Dinç the so-called *Dinç sazı*, played with the fingernails including various guitar playing techniques.

A more recent experiment in the contemporary *bağlama* tradition is the development of the *Oğur sazı* of which a six-stringed prototype was built in 1991 by Kemal Eroğlu (Kartal, Istanbul) based on a design of Erkan Oğur. In the meantime, several *Oğur sazı* types have been built, such as a thirteen-stringed and a six-stringed *Oğur sazı*. Engin Topuzkanamış (Izmir) also developed various types of the *Oğur sazı* in the meantime. Although the name *Oğur sazı* implies this long-necked lute to be a kind of *saz*, it is not. Both the playing technique, the timbre, the tuning, and the construction of the instrument are completely different. Like in the guitar playing technique, the fingernails are also used and arpeggios are played.

The continuing development of vertical and harmonic playing techniques in combination with guitar techniques, for which the *bağlama* provides the model, are of a lasting significance for Turkish folk music and the construction of long-necked lutes notwithstanding the attempts to standardization. New variants of the *bağlama* and *Oğur sazı* will undoubtedly arise in the

Figure 38. Gilad Weiss
playing a by Engin
Topuzkanamış designed and
built *Oğur sazı*.
© Courtesy Engin
Topuzkanamış, Izmir.

future. An amazing example of innovative playing techniques on the *bağlama* is demonstrated by Kemal Dinç the *Dinç sazı*, in the instrumental compositions on his CD *Bağlama için denemeler* (Exercises for *Bağlama*).[102]

A still unexplored field in Turkey to be mentioned here is the historical reproduction of Turkish long-necked lutes using historical principles of construction instead of contemporary methods. The reconstruction of historical instruments is problematical because of the scarcity of iconographic and literary sources and surviving instruments. The reproduction of traditional instruments of a more recent date present in museum and private collections is another field to be explored. One of the future goals of Engin Topuzkanamış is to explore this 'uncharted territory'.[103]

Trends in Bağlama Performance

At present, we can distinguish various trends in *bağlama* performance. Musicians such as Arif Sağ, Musa Eroğlu, Erol Parlak, and Erdal Erzincan explore new possibilities for their instruments while remaining to the existing folk musical traditions. In 2000, Erol Parlak founded the *Erol Parlak Bağlama Beşlisi* based on a 'polyphonic' approach of Anatolian folk music, from *deyiş* to *semai* and from *türküs* to *halayas* and *zeybeks*, in which the *şelpe* technique plays a central role. Erdal Erzincan demonstrates on the CD accompanying his latest book *Bağlama icin Besteler. Compositions for Baglama*, and on *Erdal Erzincan Şelpe* the high level of the contemporary *bağlama* plectrum and *şelpe* playing techniques. Emphasizing the preservation of the traditional roots of the *bağlama*, he illustrates at the same time the importance of the exploration of new ways of performance.[104]

---

[102] Dinç, K. Bağlama için denemeler (CD-DVD). Kalan CD-573.
[103] Engin Topuzkanamış. Personal communication.
[104] Erol Parlak Bağlama Beşlisi; Erzincan, E. Bağlama için Besteler. Compositions for Bağlama; Erzincan, E. Erdal Erzincan Şelpe; Erzincan, E. Bağlama için Besteler. Compositions for Bağlama: 10-12.

There are also musicians, such as the *bağlama* player Cengiz Özkan, who perform the traditional repertory on the traditional *saz*, strummed with the fingers, in pursue of a more traditional timbre for *bağlama* and voice. An amazing example are his interpretations of the songs of Âşık Veysel (*Saklarım gözümde güzelliğini*).[105]

In 1995, the *Arif Sağ Trio* was created, consisting of Arif Sağ, Erol Parlak, and Erdal Erzincan. In 1998 the *Concerto for Bağlama*, a composition by Cengiz Özdemir, was released on CD with the *İstanbul Devlet Senfoni Orkestrası* under the direction of conductor Betin Güneş. In this concert characteristic elements of folk music from Anatolia are interwoven with those of western classical music. This *Concerto for Bağlama* was also performed in Germany with the *Kölner Philharmonie* in 1996 and in the Netherlands with the *Metropole Orchestra* in 2005.

An innovative composition for *bağlama*, piano, and string quartet, *Lir ve Ateş*, combining tunes of Anatolian folk music and avant-garde improvisations was composed by the *bağlama* player Kemal Dinç. A CD-registration of this composition by Kemal Dinç (*bağlama*), Antonis Anissegos (piano), and the *Topluluğu* ensemble appeared in 2006. Kemal Dinç performed this composition during a concert tour in Germany and the Netherlands.[106]

Musicians such as Okan Murat Öztürk and his *Bengi Bağlama Üçlüsü* (Bengi Bağlama Trio) and Erkan Oğur, aim to 'modernize and enrich folk music' through the use of harmonies inspired by Kemal Ilerici (1910-1986). According to Ilerici, Anatolian folk music has a rudimentary form of polyphony, based on parallel quarters and fifths, and the use of a bourdon. He used this rudimentary polyphony, in combination with the Turkish traditional tuning, as the starting point for the design of a special harmony of Turkish folk music, which he published in 1948 under the title *Türk musîkîsi tonal sistemi ve armonisi*, a method to edit folk songs in a multi-voice way without disrupting their characteristics.

The *Bengi Bağlama* aims to implement this theory of harmony by making use of chords and harmonies for its arrangements of Anatolian folk music according to the so-called Kemal Ilerici *dörtlü armonisi sistemi* (*dörtlü*: with 4ths). In collaboration with the composer Ertuğrul Bayraktar (1951) the members of this trio are looking for possibilities to make the *bağlama* more appropriate to play chords. The *dört telli bağlama* seems to be the most suitable instrument for this. In addition, we also see that Western tonal harmony, known under the name *üçlü-beşli* (with 3rds and 5ths), is increasingly applied.[107]

Since 2010, there has been a major decline in the representation of the traditional musical styles in Turkish musical cultural tradition. The boundaries between different areas and genres of Turkish folk music have disappeared under influence of globalization and modern media, which increasingly threaten the vulnerable position of non-western traditional musical traditions and musical instruments. According to some critiques, the *bağlama* performance seems to have become an entirely show-oriented entertainment instrument that has largely lost its traditional musical and cultural context. Regional styles, musical traditions, and playing techniques that make the *bağlama* a *bağlama* moved to the background. Today's *bağlama* players

---

[105] Özkan, Ç. Saklarım gözümde güzelliğini (CD).
[106] Kemal Dinç and Chamber Musik Ensemble Drama. Lir ve Ateş. Kalan.
[107] Öztürk, O.M. A new approach in appreciating and performing the local musics. Bengi Bağlama Trio. Tradition versus change. Personal communication.

aiming to develop their own style, more and more combine traditional playing techniques with those of the *bouzoúki,* the *'ûd,* and, especially, the guitar at the cost of traditional playing styles.[108]

On the other hand, using innovative plectrum techniques, *şelpe* finger techniques and playing techniques, such as those of the guitar, opens up new ways of expressions and repertories. Notwithstanding the popularity of the guitar, this may stimulate the interest in the *bağlama* among a younger generation. An instrument which may play a central role in this process is the *Oğur sazı.* At this experimental stage it is important to keep teaching the traditional playing techniques and repertories of the *bağlama.*[109]

Migration and the Bağlama in Western Europe

Towards the end of the 1950s there was a shortage on the labour market in Western Europe. The recruitment of Turkish labour forces ('guest workers') began in the 1960s.[110] And with the labourers came also the *bağlama.* The family reunification, which started around 1973, initiated the rise of a true *bağlama* tradition in Germany, Austria, and the Netherlands. The second generation of Turks, in particular the Alevîs, wished to continue their traditions in Western Europe. At a local level, Turkish organizations started to organize *bağlama* classes. Folk musical ensembles, of which the *bağlama* was the most important instrument, emerged performing during various social events.

Since the 1990s, Turkish organizations invited well-known Turkish folk musicians to Western Europe where the *bağlama* became more widely known after the concerts of famous Turkish *bağlama* players such as Arif Sağ, Talip Özkan, Musa Eroğlu, Ali Ekber Çiçek, and Neşet Ertaş. In the Netherlands, these concerts were organized by the *Kulsan Foundation* (Kültür ve Sanat: Culture and Art), founded in 1987 by Adnan Dalkiran and Veronica Divendal. In Belgium Turkish music concerts are organized by *De Centrale* in Gent, a intercultural music centre which focuses on the organization and presentation of music mirroring the diversity of the urban population of Gent.

Among the Alevîs in Western Europe, the *bağlama* also plays an important role during religious gatherings. For the Alevîs music and dance form the core of their religious experience and identity. The *âşık* has also become a well-known figure in the Turkish communities in Western Europe. Especially in Germany with its large Turkish community, *âşıks* are substantial in the

---

[108] Okan Murat Öztürk. Personal Communication; See also Danielou, A. Die Musik Asiens zwischen Mißachtung und Wertschâtzung. Ein Beitrag zum Problem kultureller Entwicklung in der Dritten Welt.
[109] Koç, A. Bağlama-Studium am Staatlichen Konservatorium für Türkische Musik der Technischen Universität Istanbul, in Çiftçi, N. and M. Greve (eds). Die Bağlama in der Türkei und Europa. Erstes Bağlama-Symposium in Deutschland. Berlin, 14-15 September 2013: 300; Dinç, K. Bağlama-Ausbildung und der World Music Academy Codarts Rotterdam, in Çiftçi, N. and M. Greve (eds). Die Bağlama in der Türkei und Europa. Erstes Bağlama-Symposium in Deutschland. Berlin, 14-15 September 2013: 309.
[110] Uzelli Kaset was established in Frankfurt in 1971 by Muammer and Yavuz Uzelli. Their music resonated not only with the longing that Gastarbeiter (guest workers) felt for the homelands and families they had left behind and the melancholy brought by their difficult living and working conditions in Germany, but also with the joy that welled up at village weddings on their days off, and the long car or train journeys to Turkey. In 1977 they opened their Istanbul office. In the 1990s they started to release CDs. Uzelli carefully preserved its visual, audio and document archives, ensuring their survival to the present. Source: Uzelli.

Figure 39. Arif Sağ and Musa Eroğlu during a concert in the Tropeninstituut Theater
in Amsterdam.
© Courtesy Kulsan Foundation, Amsterdam.

expression of the feelings, wishes, problems, and experiences of the Turkish community in Germany.[111]

In the meantime, a generation of Turkish musicians emerged in Western Europe often having enjoyed a western conservatory education playing both Turkish and Western music, ranging from pop to jazz and rock music, on musical instruments among including the *bağlama*.[112] Following a composition assignment from the Music Meeting Foundation in 2002, the *bağlama* player, multi-instrumentalist, and composer Behsat Üvez (*d.* 2013) founded the Baraná & Co ensemble in the Netherlands. The members are from Turkey, Iran, Germany, and the Netherlands. Turkish musical forms, modern jazz, and contemporary sound experiments are the starting point of Baraná & Co.

Much has changed since the arrival of the first Turkish 'guest workers' in Western Europe. While they initially played the *bağlama* in memory of a distant homeland and *bağlama* lessons were organized by migrant organizations or social cultural institutions, much progress has been made in recent years to integrate the *bağlama* and Turkish musical traditions into the institutionalized musical cultural traditions of Western Europe, a still ongoing process.[113]

---

[111] See Kiwan, N. and U.H. Meinhof. Music and Migration: A Transnational Approach. Music and Arts in Action 3, Issue 3.
[112] Schippers, H. Facing the Musik, Shaping Music Education from a Global Perspective. Oxford: Oxford University Press.
[113] See Greve, M. Die Bağlama in Europa, in Çiftçi, N. and M. Greve (eds). Die Bağlama in der Türkei und Europa. Erstes Bağlama-Symposium in Deutschland. Berlin, 14-15 September 2013: 249-259.

Figure 40. Plaerdemavida live at Millenia studios, Valencia, September 5th, 2016. Efrén
López *Oğur sazı*, Miriam Encinas *dilruba* (seen from the back), and Meira Segal *ney*.
© Courtesy Efen López, Spain.

The government and institutions in the Netherlands have been involved into multicultural
musical practices and musical education since the early 1980s. In the major cities, world music
departments have been set up at municipal music schools since 1990. The *bağlama* classes, for
which Turkish teachers were attracted, occupy an important place in the education of Turkish
music. The establishment in 2000 of a *bağlama* college at the Hogeschool voor Muziek en Dans in
Rotterdam to take *bağlama* training to a higher level was an important and unique development
at that time. In 2005 this college continued under the name *Codarts* (Co(nservatoire), da(nce)
and arts) at the Rotterdam Academy for World.[114]

In Germany, the *bağlama* is also taught at private and municipal music schools in Germany is of a
higher level. In 2015, a study program World Music with the *bağlama*, Arab and Turkish *'ûd*, and
Middle Eastern percussion started at the Popakademie in Baden-Würtenberg in cooperation
with the Oriental Music Academy Mannheim. A certificate course for the training of *bağlama*
teachers was initiated by the University of Music and Dance in Cologne in cooperation with the
Landesmusikakademie Nordrhein-Westfalen. In 2016, the first student in music education with
the *bağlama* as main subject started at the Berlin University of Art. In other areas, however, the
bağlama is still underrepresented in the German musical traditions.[115]

[114] Dinç, K. Bağlama-Ausbildung and der World Music Academy Codarts Rotterdam, in Çiftçi, N. and M. Greve (eds). Die
Bağlama in der Türkei und Europa. Erstes Bağlama-Symposium in Deutschland. Berlin, 14-15 September 2013: 306.
[115] Greve, M. Die Bağlama in Europa, in Çiftçi, N. and M. Greve (eds). Die Bağlama in der Türkei und Europa. Erstes

Figure 41. Kemal Dinç playing a *Dinç sazı*.
© Courtesy Kemal Dinç.

In Switzerland, Basel has a lively Turkish musical life and the *bağlama* education is, like in Germany, of a high standard. Developments in Belgium are lagging behind. The education of Turkish music in which the *bağlama* takes a central position is organized by municipalities and Turkish organizations, whether or not subsidized by the government. In musical life and musical education the *bağlama* is still underrepresented. In Austria, the *bağlama* is hardly integrated in musical life. Many Turkish associations in Vienna and federal states of Austria teach *bağlama* and other folk musical instruments of Turkey to which outsiders have no access with the exception to the *bağlama* courses of Mansur Bildik, a situation mirroring the level of integration.[116]

The Bağlama in the 21st Century

Despite the increasing popularity of the guitar, the *bağlama* is still popular among Turkish the youth in Turkey and Western Europe. However, its future, in Turkey as well as Europe, depends on the question whether the *bağlama* is only an instrument of a certain musical cultural tradition or whether it can ''emancipate' itself from its cultural roots, like the guitar from its Iberian roots, and become a musical instrument in its own right".[117]

Bağlama-Symposium in Deutschland. Berlin, 14-15 September 2013: 250-256.
[116] Sels, L. Türkische Volksmusik und die Bağlama in Gent (Belgien), in Çiftçi, N. and M. Greve (eds) Die Bağlama in der Türkei und Europa. Erstes Bağlama-Symposium in Deutschland. Berlin, 14-15 September 2013: 233-242: Sağlam, H. Musikalische Vermittlungsmöglichkeiten von Migrantinnen aus der Türkei in Österreich/Wien, in Çiftçi, N. and M. Greve (eds). Die Bağlama in der Türkei und Europa. Erstes Bağlama-Symposium in Deutschland. Berlin, 14-15 September 2013: 217-231.
[117] See for discussion Betton, J. Die Bağlama als Teil der Hochschulausbidung in Deutschland? in Çiftçi, N. and M. Greve (eds). Die Bağlama in der Türkei und Europa. Erstes Bağlama-Symposium in Deutschland. Berlin, 14-15 September 2013.

Musicians which are key figures in establishing the *bağlama* as an instrument in its own right in Turkey are musicians such as Erkan Oğur, Kemal Dinç, especially on the CD *Bağlama için Denemeler* (Exercises for Bağlama), and Ahmet Aslan exploring new ways of expression, sounds, and playing techniques initiating new *bağlama* types such as the *Oğur sazı* and the *Dinç sazı*, already mentioned, and the *guitar-saz*, a hybrid of a *saz* (neck) and guitar (body), built by the luthier Süleyman Aslan.[118] While for some playing techniques, repertory, and construction of the *bağlama* advanced significantly, for others, however, the *bağlama* is moving away from its roots.

Outside Turkey, musicians such as Efrén López in Spain and Gilad Weiss in Israel contribute to the establishment of the *bağlama* and the *Oğur sazı* as fully-fledged solo and ensemble instruments.[119] As a multi-instrumentalist and composer Efrén López is an example of a musician performing in various crossover ensembles blending European with non-European musical traditions, including the use of the Turkish long-necked lutes.

---

[118] Dinç, K. Bağlama için Denemeler (CD+DVD); Aslan, A. and K. Dinç. Duo (CD).
[119] López, E. El Fill del Llop; Jota Martínez Ensemble. Instrumentos Musicales de la Tradición Medieval Española. Musical Instruments of the Spanish Medieval Tradition.

Chapter-2
Variation versus Standardization

In the past there existed a variety of regional and local Turkish long-necked lutes of which many have been lost, forgotten or fallen into oblivion. These long-necked lutes had in general three individual strings made of gut and 6, 12 or 17 movable frets which were also made of gut. Since the early years of the Republic of Turkey, Turkish long-necked lutes have been increasingly modified and standardized resulting around the 1980s in the *bağlama* family (*bağlama ailesi*).[120] The Turkish long-necked lute tradition is, notwithstanding the loss of the many regional and local variations and process of modification and standardization, still very rich and varied to this day due to the continuing development of new versions of the *bağlama*.

The long-necked lutes of the *bağlama* family have a number of characteristics in common.

- A pear-shaped bowl (*tekne, gövde*) and a generally under the tailpiece (*alt eşik, tel bağlama takozu*) located sound hole (*kafes*).
- A slightly arched wooden soundboard (*göğüs, kapak*).
- A narrow long neck (*sap*) with tied-on movable nylon frets (*perde*) ending into a slightly angled neck (*eğmeli burguluk*) with four laterally and three frontally positioned wooden pegs (*düzen burguları*).
- A movable bridge (*alt eşik*) clamped between the strings and the soundboard.
- In courses, double or triple, closely grouped strings which are played as one string to increase the volume and enrich the tone. The strings of a course are tuned to the same notes. On contemporary *bağlamas*, one of the strings on the first and third courses and sometimes also of the second course has been replaced by a so-called *bam teli* or octave string. This in copper or silver wire wrapped string, which was introduced on the *saz* by Neşet Ertaş towards the end of the 1950s, is tuned one octave lower.[121] The strings run from the tailpiece at the rim of the bowl over the movable bridge on the soundboard via the nut (*üst eşik*), located at the transition between neck and pegbox, to the tuning pegs.
- In general twenty-four frets. Calculated over the three string groups, the range of instruments of the *bağlama* family is two octaves. The short-necked *bağlama* (*kısa saplı bağlama*), a variant of the long-necked *bağlama* (*uzun saplı bağlama*), with nineteen frets is an exception to this. Calculated over the three string groups, the range of the short-necked *bağlama* is a tredicime (octave plus a sext).

The Bağlama Family

The long-necked lutes of the *bağlama* family are classified in various ways by Turkish scholars, musicians, and luthiers. Among academics, *bağlama* players, and luthiers circulate several

---

[120] See Parlak, E. Standardization of the bağlama and the development of its notation from the founding of the republic to the present, in Çiftçi, N. and M. Greve (eds) Die Bağlama in der Türkei und Europa. Erstes Bağlama-Symposium in Deutschland. Berlin, 14-15 September 2013: 63-102.
[121] Neşet Ertaş. Personal communication. According to another source, Bayram Aracı and Orhan Subay also played a role in the introduction of the bam teli.

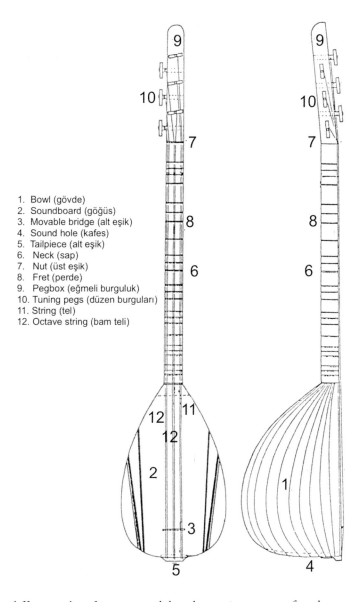

Figure 42. *Bağlamanın Anatomisi* (Anatomy Bağlama).
© Courtesy Cafer Açın, Istanbul.

1. Bowl (gövde)
2. Soundboard (göğüs)
3. Movable bridge (alt eşik)
4. Sound hole (kafes)
5. Tailpiece (alt eşik)
6. Neck (sap)
7. Nut (üst eşik)
8. Fret (perde)
9. Pegbox (eğmeli burguluk)
10. Tuning pegs (düzen burguları)
11. String (tel)
12. Octave string (bam teli)

different classification models. The main reasons for these various classification are the richness and variety in names, sizes and shapes, the continuing development of new *bağlama* types, and theoretical and personal disagreements.[122]

A definite and consistent classification of musical instruments taking into account not only contemporary instruments but also those of the past is almost a mission impossible. Many classification systems have been tried in the course of time. There are a large number of well-

---

[122] See for further discussion Terzi, C. Klassifizierung der in Anatolien gespielten Baplama-Familie in terminologischer, typologischer und tonräumlicher Hinsicht, in Çiftçi, N. and M. Greve (eds) Die Bağlama in der Türkei und Europa. Erstes Bağlama-Symposium in Deutschland. Berlin, 14-15 September 2013: 17-36.

known, standardized forms, and a wealth of hybrid and transitional forms. Another problem is confusing variation in the naming of instruments, mainly due to ethnic, geographical, and linguistic factors.

The development and establishment of a generally accepted nomenclature and systematic classification of Turkish long-necked lutes, not being part of this study, still has to be undertaken. It goes without saying, that such a nomenclature and classification, although by definition debatable, is an indispensable diagnostic tool in any scientific research of musical instruments.[123]

Around the 1940s, Turkish long-necked lutes, such as the *bozuk* with five or six strings, the *bağlama* with four, six, and eight strings, the *yalağı* with four strings, the *şarkı* with six strings, the *kövür* or *çövür* with eight or twelve strings, the *bulgarı* with three strings, *çağur* with six or nine strings, *ırızva* or *karadüzen* with three strings, *baltı sazı* with three or seven strings, and the five or seven-stringed *baz-bağlama* were mentioned or discussed in various literary sources, however, not in the context of a classification model.[124]

Since the 1960s, Turkish long-necked lutes are discussed in the context of a classification model:

- Adnan Ataman. (1926-1992) distinguished in 1961, from small to large, the *cura*, *bağlama*, *cura bağlama* or *tambura*, *bozuk*, *divan sazı* (audience hall *saz*), and *meydan sazı* (public-square *saz*).
- Richard Campbell distinguished in 1968, from small to large, the *cura*, *bulgaria*, *bağlama*, *bozuk*, *divan sazı*, and *meydan sazı*.
- Cafer Açın (1939-2012) distinguished in 1994, from small to large, the *tanbura curası* (bowl 22,5 cm, neck 30 cm, mensur 48 cm, width and depth bowl 13,5 cm) *bağlama curası* (bowl 26,5 cm, neck 35 cm, mensur 56 cm, width and depth bowl 15,5 cm), *tanbura* (bowl 38 cm, neck 50 cm, mensur 80 cm, width and depth bowl 22,8 cm), *bağlama* (bowl 42 cm, neck 55 cm, mensur 88 cm, width and depth bowl 25 cm), *divan sazı* (bowl 49 cm, neck 65 cm, mensur 104 cm, width and depth bowl 29,5 cm), and *meydan sazı* (bowl 52,5 cm, neck 70 cm, mensur 112 cm, width and depth bowl 31,5 cm). 'Golden ratios' (*enstrumanlarda altın oranlar*) govern the construction and on frequency ratios based tuning of the frets (*frekans ve perde aralıkları*) in the classification of Cafer Açın.[125]
- The *bağlama* player and author Erol Parlak distinguishes, from small to large, the *tambura curası* (length bowl 31-33 cm), the *bağlama curası* (length bowl 33-36 cm), the *tambura* (length bowl 39-40 cm), the *bağlama* (length bowl 45-46 cm), the *divan sazı* (length bowl 51-52 cm), and the *meydan sazı* (length bowl 55-56 cm).[126]

---

[123] See for discussion Wachsmann, K., M.J. Kartomi, E.M. van Horbostel and C. Sachs. Instruments, classification of: 418-428; Picken, L. Folk Musical Instruments of Turkey: 558-570.

[124] Picken, L. Folk Musical Instruments of Turkey: 209; Campbell, R.G. Zur Typologie der Schalenlanghalslaute: 276-278.

[125] Picken, L. Folk Musical Instruments of Turkey: 209; Campbell, R.G. Zur Typologie der Schalenlanghalslaute: 49-70; Açın, Cafer. Bağlama. Yapım sanatı ve sanatçıları: 32-33.

[126] Parlak, E. Standardization of the bağlama and the development of its notation from the founding of the republic to the present, in Çiftçi, N. and M. Greve (eds) Die Bağlama in der Türkei und Europa. Erstes Bağlama-Symposium in Deutschland. Berlin, 14-15 September 2013: 90.

- The *bağlama* player and author Okan Murat Öztürk distinguishes, from small to large, the *cura* (length 23-30 cm), the *bağlama* (length 32-36 cm), *tambura* (length 38-42 cm), *çöğür* (length 44-46 cm), and *divan sazı* (length 48-52 cm).[127]
- Cihangir Terzi concludes in 2013 that there seems to be a consensus in classifying the *bağlama* family into three main categories, a *cura* group (from small to large consisting of the *parmak curası*, *dört telli cura* (*bulgarı*, *karadüzen*), *dede curası* (*ruzva*, *ırızva*), and *bağlama curası*, a *tambura/bağlama* group (from small to large consisting of the *çöğür curası* or *cura bağlama*, *tambura* with a short or long neck, *bağlama*, and *âşık sazı* or *abdal sazı*), and a *divan* group (from small to large consisting of the *kırkbeşlık saz* or *bozuk*, *ğöğür* or *yetik* or *divan ufağı*, *divan sazı*, *büyük divan sazı* or *meydan sazı*.[128]

A possible classification of the *bağlama* family is, ranging from small to large, the *cura*, short-necked *bağlama* (*kısa saplı bağlama*), long-necked *bağlama* (*uzun-saplı bağlama*), *tambura*, *divan sazı*, and *meydan sazı*. *Bağlamas* not included in the *bağlama* family, such as the *dört telli bağlama* (four-course *bağlama*), the *perdesiz tanbura* (fretless *tanbura*), the *electro bass bağlama* (electric bass *bağlama*), the *semi-akustik bağlama* (semi-acoustic *bağlama*), and the *Oğur sazı* and its variations, are discussed in section *Variation versus Standardization*.[129]

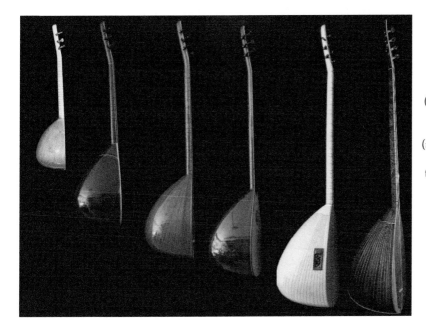

Figure 43. The *bağlama family* consisting of the *cura*, the short-necked *bağlama* (*kısa saplı bağlama*) and the long-necked *bağlama* (*uzun saplı bağlama*) and, the *tambura*, the *divan sazı*, and the *meydan sazı*. © Author.

---

[127] Öztürk, O.M. A new approach in appreciating and performing the local musics. Bengi Bağlama Trio. Tradition versus change. Personal communication.
[128] Çiftçi, N. Klassifizierung der in Anatolien gespieten Bağlama-Famile in terminologischer, typologischer und tonräumlicher Hinsicht in Çiftçi, N. and M. Greve (eds) 2017. Die Bağlama in der Türkei und Europa. Erstes Bağlama-Symposium in Deutschland. Berlin, 14-15 September 2013: 19-21.
[129] See for discussion classification of musical instruments Wachsmann K, Kartomi MJ, Hornbostel EM von, Sachs, C. Classification of Instruments.

The Cura

The cura (Persian for drop, nip or little) is the smallest instrument from the *bağlama* family. According to Jérôme Cler (*Le baglama de yayla*), the *cura* or small *bağlama* belongs to the same two or three-stringed lutes as the Turkmen *dutâr*, the Kyrgyz *komuz*, and the *dömbra* of Kazakhstan.

The *cura* is played with a plectrum or with the fingers, especially in the Aegean and southern Turkey. An important player on this instrument was Ramazan Güngör (1924-2004) from Fethiye, who played the *cura* with his fingers (*şelpe* finger technique). When Erol Parlak started working in 1988 on the further development of the *şelpe technique* and in particular the *parmak vurma* technique (a kind of hammering on the strings), he also visited Ramazan Güngör in Fethiye, whose playing technique he recorded on film. Tunings for the cura used by Ramazan Güngör include the *zeybek düzeni* (I:a, II:d, III:g), the *bağlama düzeni* (I:a, II:d, III:e) and the *bozuk düzeni* (I:a, II:e, III:b). I is the highest sounding course, II the middle course, and III the lowest sounding string.

The *cura*, also called *üç telli kopuz* or *üç telli bağlama* by the farmers, was originally a two to three-stringed lute with ten to eighteen frets. The old two-string *cura* with twelve frets, symbolizing the twelve imams, was also called the *dede curası*, because it was played during religious ceremonies of the Alevî by the *dede* (spiritual father), or *parmak curası* because he was strummed with fingers, although in a different style than Ramazan Göngür.

Figure 44. Hayrı Dev (*d.* 2018) from Gökçeyaka (south-western Turkey) playing a *üç telli bağlama*.
© Courtesy Jérôme Cler, France.

The *üç telli bağlama* played by the charismatic Hayri Dev (1933-2018) is an example of a small simple *saz*. An interesting detail is the from a single piece of wood carved 'teeth-like' tailpiece (*dip eşik*) under the rim of the bowl. In the past, the strings were also looped around a 'teeth-like' tailpiece that had been cut from the *oyma* bowl, as is also the case here. The *üç telli bağlama* from Hayri Dev has a one-piece soundboard. Most of the small long-necked lutes on the Anatolian countryside had a flat and one-piece soundboard.[130]

The Bağlama

The contemporary long-necked *bağlama* is, like the other lutes of the *bağlama* family, a result of the morphological changes of Turkish long-necked lutes after 1960. The increasing combination of the traditional horizontal playing technique with vertical playing techniques

---

[130] Picken, L. Folk Musical Instruments of Turkey: 216, 221.

on the long-necked *bağlama* tuned in *bağlama düzeni*, resulted around the 1980s in the short-necked *bağlama*. In order to make more effective use of the vertical possibilities and *bağlama düzeni*, the neck was shortened, *decreasing* the distance between the tonal intervals.

It was in particular Arif Sağ who put, besides Yavuz Top, Hasret Gültekin (1971-1993), and Musa Eroğlu, the short-necked *bağlama* on the map around the 1980s inspiring a younger generation of *bağlama* players. He succeeded in boosting the emotional impact of his playing through sophisticated plectrum movements and ornamentations with the left hand. An example is his virtuoso *Teke Zortlaması*.[131] Around 2000, the short-necked *bağlama* lost its influence. Notwithstanding its popularity, the short-necked *bağlama* has not replaced the long-necked *bağlama*.

The Tambura

The *tambura* (*tanbura*) forms the transition to the larger lutes from the *bağlama* family, the *divan sazı* and the *meydan sazı*. Some *tambura* types are specific to West Anatolia, others to Central Anatolia. Depending on the region, the *tambura* is also called *saz*, *bağlama*, *bozuk* or *çöğür*.

The old *tamburas* differ from the contemporary *tamburas* in construction, tuning, number, and arrangement of frets and strings. There is a large regional variation. Old *tamburas* have a cone-shaped bowl without sound hole, a straight neck, and a curved soundboard.

The tuning and way of playing of the *tambura* is, like that of the long-necked *bağlama*, *bozuk düzeni* and horizontally up and down the neck of the first string group. The *tanbura* has seven strings divided into three choirs, including octave strings, which are only plucked with a plectrum. Some musicians prefer to replace the upper string of the middle string group with an octave string. On some old *tamburas*, the third string group consists of three strings (two steel strings and an octave string (3+2+3 or 3+3+3).

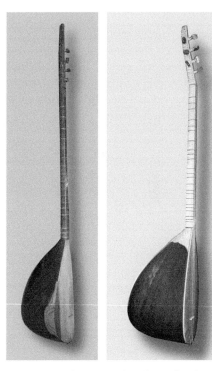

Figure 45. Eight-stringed traditional and seven-stringed contemporary *tambura*.
© Author.

The Divan Sazı

The *divan sazı* (audience-hall *saz*) is the accompanying instrument of the âşıks. The *divan sazı* probably owes its name to the habit of playing the instrument sitting cross-legged on a long and low cushioned couch (*divan*) also indicating the size of this large long-necked lute.

---

[131] Turkish Folk Songs and Instrumental Music, King Records, registration 2.

The *divan sazı* has three string groups and twenty-four frets. The first string group consists of two steel strings of 0.30 mm, the middle string group of a steel string of 0.20 mm and an octave string (*bam teli*) of 0.45/0.50 mm, the third string group of a steel string of 0.30/0.32 mm and an octave string (*bam teli*) of 0.70/0.80 mm. The *divan sazı* is generally tuned in *bozuk düzeni* and is played with a plectrum.

The Meydan Sazı

The *meydan sazı* (public-square *saz*) is the largest *saz* of the *bağlama* family. In *La musique Turque*, Rauf Yekta called the *meydan sazı âşık sazı*, the *saz* of the *âşık*. The word *meydan*, Turkish for square or place, is also an indication of the format of this instrument. The powerful sound makes the *meydan sazı* ideal for playing in large spaces or outdoors. The story goes that the *meydan sazı* was during the Ottoman Empire used in military actions to encourage the soldiers and frighten the enemy.

The *meydan sazı* has the same characteristics as the *divan sazı*. The strings and tuning of the *meydan sazı* are the same as that of the *divan sazı* and can be adjusted to the wishes of the player. Professional players have an octave string (*bam teli*) in each string group, making the instrument sounding like a bass. Due to the large intervals between the frets on the neck of both the *meydan sazı* and the *divan sazı*, playing on these lutes is less fast and the number of ornamentations is limited. Nowadays, the *meydan sazı* has become a rare and on commission built instrument.

Ali Ekber Çiçek (1934-2006) was a well-known virtuoso on both the *divan* and *meydan sazı*.[132] *On dört yıl dolandım Pervânelikte* (Fourteen years I wandered in the moth's orbit, Bektaşi *türkü*) of the 14th-century of the 14th-century Sûfî poet Sıtkı (Sıtkı Baba) inspired Ali Ekber Çiçek to compose *On dört bin yıl gezdim pervanelikte* (I wandered for fourteen thousand years), an innovative composition which accompanying himself on the *divan sazı* or *meydan sazı* (1965).[133]

On dört yıl dolandım Pervânelikte	Fourteen years I wandered in the moth's orbit
Sıtkı ismin aldım dîvânelikte	Fidelity[1] was the name that I adopted
İçtim şarabını mestânelikte	I drank your wine in the abode of drunkenness
Kırkların ceminde dara düş oldum	In the congregation of the Forty Saints
Kırkların ceminde Haydar Haydar dara düş oldum	I was challenged crying Haydar Haydar[2]
Gürûh-ı Nâcî'ye özümü kattım	I added my soul into the Band of the Salvaged
Âdem sıfatıyla çok geldim gittim	I frequented it freely as Âdem[3]
Bülbül oldum Firdevs bağında öttüm	I was a nightingale singing in the Garden of Eden
Bir zaman gül için zara düş oldum	I wept copiously after the rose for a while
Kırkların ceminde Haydar Haydar dara düş oldum	In the congregation crying Haydar Haydar[134]

[1]Fidelity = Sıtkı; [2]Haydar = Lion-Harted; [3]Âdem = Adam.

---

[132] Turkey – Bektashi Musik. Ashik Songs. Registration 12.
[133] Haydar ('lion-hearted'), nickname of Ali, the son in law of the Prophet.
[134] Translated by Engin D. Akarlı and Gülay Yurdal-Michael.

Figure 46. Ali Ekber Çicek.
© Unknown source.

In his composition, Ali Ekber Çiçek explores the technical and harmonic possibilities of the *divan sazı/meydan sazı*, of which the complex rhythmic patterns and new plectrum techniques attract attention. The instrumental prelude is performed by many *bağlama* players to demonstrate their virtuosity such as *Haydar Haydar* played by Okan Murat Öztürk on the *dört telli bağlama* and Coşkun Gülâ on a *saz*.[135]

Variation versus Standardization

A new generation of *bağlamas* evolved since the 1980s such as the *dört telli bağlama* (four-course *bağlama*), the *perdesiz tanbura* (fretless *tanbura*), the *electro bass bağlama* (*electric bass bağlama*), the *semi akustik bağlama* (*semi-acoustic bağlama*) and the by Erkan Oğur designed *Oğur sazı* on which *bağlama* players experimented with new playing techniques and timbre. Moreover, the acoustic *bağlama*, became popular again since the 1990s among producers who were looking for a more traditional style and timbre.

The systematic use of all strings or string groups, to minimize the number of movements along the neck on the first string group, was an important feature of the playing technique in the city. On the *dört telli bağlama* and *Oğur sazı* we see an increase in the vertical and harmonic playing techniques by expanding the number of strings or string groups. The *dört telli bağlama*, built for Okan Murat Öztürk by Murtaza Çağır in 1996, is used by him for harmonic purposes and to play melodic patterns in different tunings.

The first *Oğur sazı* built by Kemal Eroğlu based on a design of Erkan Oğur, is a new experiment in the Turkish long-necked tradition. To increase the vertical and in particular harmonic possibilities, the number of strings or string groups was expanded. The first six-stringed prototype from 1991 was followed by a number of variations, including a thirteen-stringed

---

[135] Çiçek, A.E. Turkish Sufi Music. Folk Lute of Anatolia.Registration 9. Okan Murat Öztürk. Turkish Authentic Saz, registration 12; Coşkun Gülâ. Bağlamada Tezene Tavırları, registration 4.

Figure 47. Prototype *Oğur sazı* (left). Erkan Oğur playing a *on üç telli Oğur sazı* (six-course: 3-2-2-2-2-2, middle). *Altı telli Oğur sazı* (six-stringed, right).
© Author.

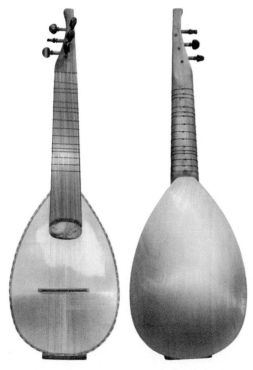

Figure 48. Six-stringed flat-backed 'mandolin version' of the *Oğur sazı* by Engin Topuzkanamış.
© Author/Engin Topuzkanamış, Izmir.

(five double-stringed courses and one triple-stringed course) and a six-stringed version. According to Kemal Eroğlu, the *Oğur sazı* has found its ideal form in the meantime. The six-stringed version gives, according to him, the best result in terms of sound and playing technique possibilities.

Kemal Eroğlu and Erkan Oğur are furthermore experimenting with drop-shaped bowls. In combination with steel strings, this shape would, at least according to Erkan Oğur, lend itself better to the *şelpe* playing technique. This long-necked lute, named *kopuz* by them, is built in a long or short-necked version.

The development of the *Oğur sazı* and its establishment in the Turkish musical culture is still ongoing. The *Oğur sazı* was, since the six-stringed version, also built by various other luthiers. The luthier and musician Engin Topuzkanamış (Izmir) is probably the most innovative one of them, experimenting with a variety of *Oğur sazı* designs such as a 'mandolin' version of the *Oğur sazı*.

In the meantime he built *Oğur sazı* versions for musicians such as Efrén López and Guillermo Rizotto in Spain, and Gilad Weiss in Israel. The most recent version, a hybrid of the European lute and *Oğur sazı*, was designed and built by him on request of Gilad Weiss.

Figure 49. Ten-stringed *Oğur sazı* and six-stringed '*kopuz*' version of the Oğur sazı by Engin Topzkanımış.
© Author/Engin Topuzkanamış, Izmir.

Chapter-3
Construction

Long-necked lutes are made and played since ancient times undergoing in the meantime various morphological changes when different musical and tonal demands were imposed on them. Originally being small two-stringed long-necked lutes (*tanbûrs*), they evolved in the course of time into more sophisticated instruments with two or more, occasionally doubled or tripled courses, and a varying number of variously tuned frets and strings. Besides the ancient one-piece design, a composite design probably evolved in the course time in imitation of the *'ûd* according to which the neck is attached to a carved-hollowed-out or carvel-built bowl.[136]

Despite the far-reaching degree of mechanization, lute making in Turkey is still a traditional activity of individual luthiers in small workshops. In the past, musicians and common people in rural Anatolia often built their own instruments. Instruments are furthermore built in series and mass production, particularly in Istanbul and the other major cities in Turkey. High-quality instruments are, however, only built in small numbers in workshops. Beside using the traditional tools, some luthiers more recently started to use power carving tools such as an angle grinder or even CNC-machines, a manufacturing process in which pre-programmed computer software dictates the movement of factory tools and machinery to perform milling, drilling, taping, and sawing.[137]

The development of national musical cultures in the Republic of Turkey and Central Asian Soviet republics in the 20th century included the modification and standardization of the long-necked *tanbûrs*.[138] A number of universities and conservatories in Turkey, Uzbekistan, and Kazakhstan have departments of instrument design where the construction of instruments is approached and taught to future luthiers in a more academic manner that seeks to improve and standardize instrument construction. Outside this academic context, however, the musical practice continues to dictate the construction of musical instruments.

In Turkey the academic education of instrument construction dates back to the establishment of an Instrument Manufacturing Workshop at the Ankara State Conservatory in 1936. The modification and standardization of Uzbek musical instruments, dating back to the 1920s and early 1930s, primarily focuses on the improvement of the construction of instrument, sound amplification, and the expansion of the tonal range by adding more frets tuned to the European twelve-tone equal temperament.

In particular Cafer Açın (1939-2012), the former head of the instrument section of the State Conservatory in Istanbul (Enstruman Yapım Bölümü Başkanı, Türk Müziği Devlet Konservatuarı, Istanbul Teknik Üniversitesi), has attempted to standardize instrument making in Turkey. Several books about instrument construction appeared from his hand. In *Bağlama. Yapım sanatı ve sanatçıları*, he introduces a standard construction method and number and tuning of

---

[136] Djani-Zade, T. Die organologische und ikonographische Gestalt der türkischen Lauten. Über das historische Zupfinstrument qâpâz-i ôz: 71.
[137] Engin Topuzkanamış. Personal communication.
[138] Blum, S. Central Asia: 363-365.

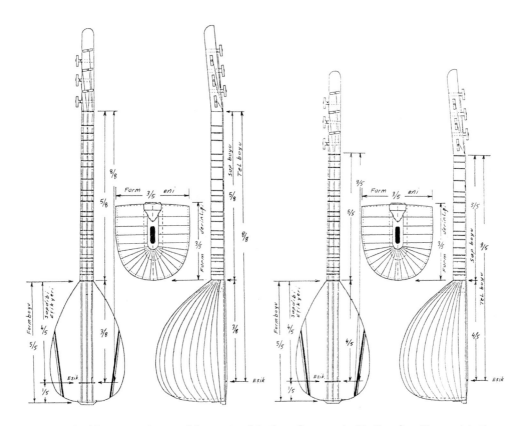

Figure 50. 'Golden Section' rates of the *uzun saplı bağlama* (long-necked *bağlama*) and *kısa saplı bağlama* (short-necked *bağlama*) by Cafer Açin.
© Courtesy Cafer Açın, Istanbul.

frets and strings of the various long-necked lutes of the *bağlama* family. 'Golden Section' rates governing the construction of these instruments and the arithmetically established frequency ratios of the positioning of the frets reflect this academic attitude. In practice, however, we see that instrument construction is determined by the musical practice.[139]

The Choice of Wood

Different types of wood are used to make a *bağlama*. Deciduous wood is used for the bowl and conifer wood for the soundboard, preferably pine or spruce (*çam ağacı* or *ladin ağacı*). The wood of the bowl and soundboard must be free of knots. Neck, pegbox, tuning pegs, nut and bridge are made of hardwood: oak, beech, mahogany or plum (*meşe ağacı, gürgen ağacı, maun*, and *erik ağacı*). Since a number of wood species are scarce or hardly available, exotic wood species, of which mahogany is commonly used since it is relatively less expensive, are also imported and used.[140]

---

[139] Açın, C. Enstruman Bilimi. Açın C. Bağlama. Yapım Sanatı ve Sanatçıları.
[140] Engin Topuzkanamış. Personal communication.

Trees that grow at high altitudes and under difficult conditions, such as cold weather and a poor soil, are excellent. The wood of these trees is hard (small cells of the same size) and therefore has a good resonance. Wood from trees grown under favourable conditions in rich soil is soft, large cells of unequal size, and therefore less resonant. Soft woods are not as strong as hard woods and therefore bend more over time in combination with the string traction.

Trees suitable for instrument construction, of which only the knot-free parts are used, are usually harvested between mid-October and mid-November when the sap flow stops. Processing takes place between January and April.

The Drying of Wood

Essential for the construction of a good instrument is that the wood used is well dried and worked out, resulting in an instrument that is more resistant to large differences in temperature and humidity. In addition, the manner in which the wood is dried is also important. Wood that has been dried naturally, in a room with proper ventilation and temperature, or that has been exposed to the temperature and humidity conditions of the changing seasons, leads to better results than artificially dried wood.

Naturally dried wood is 'alive' and considered to be superior as drying the wood in an kiln (oven) 'kills' the wood. Kiln-dried wood (*fırın kurutma*) reduces the humidity level to 6-8% in a very short time. However, after taking the wood out of the kiln it absorbs humidity from its environment again and its humidity level becomes equal with the outside. So it doesn't matter if the wood is natural or kiln-dried. The problem with kiln-dried wood is, however, that drying goes so fast that it causes 'internal stress' in the wood. More recently there are, although not in Turkey, some new drying techniques such as torrefaction, being a thermal treatment of wood at temperatures of 200 to 300°C in the absence of oxygen. Storage times vary, some think ten years is ideal for the soundboard and two to three years or longer for the bowl. Others believe one can make excellent instruments with just two years old woods.

The vast majority of instrument makers cannot afford a long storage time for wood because of the costs involved. For this reason, wood is dried in an kiln. Factory-built instruments are often made of kiln-dried wood, instruments build by master luthiers or in small workshops generally not.

Construction Process

A luthier has a building strategy in mind. The starting point is the type, design, and types of wood used for the various parts of the instrument.[141] The order of the construction process is always the same: bowl, neck and pegbox, and soundboard, although some luthiers first glue the soundboard and then the neck, after which the instrument is polished (gloss or matt) and the tuning pegs, nut, frets, and bridge and strings are installed.

---

[141] See Picken, L. Folk Musical Instruments of Turkey: 273-275.

Figure 51. Stages construction process *Oğur sazı*.
© Courtesy Engin Topuzkanamış, Izmir.

Bowl

The pear-shaped bowl (or belly) is made in two different ways: carved-hollowed-out from a block of wood (*oyma*) or composed of ribs (*yapraklı, dilimli*). The types of wood used for *oyma* include mulberry (*dut ağacı*), chestnut (*kestane ağacı*), alder (*kızıl ağaç*), elm (*kara ağaç*), beech (*gürgen ağacı*), and lime (*ıhlamur ağacı*).

Depending on the size of the instrument, the tree trunk is halved or quartered lengthwise. In the first case, the bowl is hollowed out from the heart of the tree and in the second case from the outside to the heart of the tree. When using a half tree trunk, the annual rings of the wood follow the bulging of the bowl, so that they are strong where needed: around the junction the neck and the bowl, at the tailpiece, and the sound hole.

Figure 52. Carved-hollowed-out bowl (*oyma*) and carvel-built bowl (*yapraklı*).
© Author.

A template is used to mark the profile of the bowl. Carving, hollowing-out and determining the correct thickness of the bowl is a labour-intensive process. For a better resonance: the thinner the better. Incidentally, it is not unusual for luthiers to have the bowl manufactured by specialists (*oymacı*).[142]

---

[142] Enging Topuzkanımış. Personal communication.

   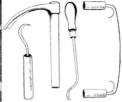

Figure 53. Carving and hollowing-out the bowl from a block of wood. Tools used to hollow-out the bowl: the large axe is used for carving and hollowing out bowl, the curved gauges for curving in depth, and the scrapper for smoothing the surface of the bowl.
© Courtesy Engin Topuzkanamış, Izmir.

The thickness of the bowl is also determined by the type of wood and its properties and is not the same everywhere. The bowl is thicker at the junction of the neck and the bowl, the tailpiece, and the sound hole. The keel or bottom of the bowl is the thinnest part. A V-shaped joint is cut into the heel of the bowl, into which the neck is glued. In the case of oyma, the tailpiece, made of boxwood (şimşir ağacı), is glued under the rim of the bowl.

In order to increase the sound volume, a round sound hole is sawn under the tailpiece for some forty years. Old sazs had no sound hole, but small soundholes in the bowl as well as soundboard. The meydan sazıs in the folk music orchestras of Radio Ankara and Radio Istanbul formed one exception. They had a sound hole under the tailpiece with a hatch (ahenk kapağı) that could be opened or closed enhancing the treble, or closed, suppressing the bass and reducing the sound volume.

A bowl without sound hole(s) reinforces the high tones, suppresses bass, and reduces the volume. The cura of Gaziantep (south-eastern Anatolia) had a small round sound hole in the middle of the soundboard.[143] Contemporary bağlamas are sometimes, among others by the luthier Süleyman Aslan, executed with a sound hole in the soundboard using a bracing system to support the soundboard. Old Anatolian lutes often had one or more small soundholes in the soundboard and/or left side of the bowl. They can still be found in the bowl and/or soundboard of Central Asian tanbûrs.

Some old oyma bowls had a conical-shaped bowl (konik tekne, balık sırtı, balta gibi), a design feature which can also be found on the Balkan. There are luthiers who believe that the conical shape belonged to an older tradition, especially in Gaziantep and the surrounding area, others believe that it was characteristic of Central and Eastern Anatolia.[144] One sometimes also mentioned possibility is that this conical, sometimes, almost V-shaped dorsal ridge of the bowl made it possible for the Alevî dedes to sit for hours on their knees while playing during their religious ceremonies.

The idea to build a bowl consisting of ribs originated in the Arab world and evolved from the demand for instruments with a high resonance. The first mentioning of a bowl made of ribs (carvel-built) can be found in the Ikhwân al-Safa (Brothers of purity), a collection of scientific and philosophical Arabic texts from the 10th century. How far this tradition goes back is

---

[143] Picken, L. Folk Musical Instruments of Turkey: 220.
[144] Picken, L. Folk Musical Instruments of Turkey: 278-279.

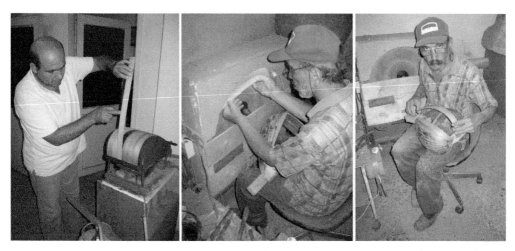

Figure 54. Süleyman Fırtına bending the ribs using a bending iron after which the ribs are customized and assembled on a mold, Fırtına Müzikevi, Istanbul.
© Author.

unknown, but there are indications that this construction method was already known to the Arabs in the 9th and possibly even towards the end of the 8th century. The pumpkin with its rib pattern may have been the model for building a bowl made of ribs. This made it possible - in comparison with instruments with a carved-hollowed-out bowl - to build lighter instruments with a high resonance. The ribbing technique is one of the skills introduced in Europe from the Arab world in Europe in the Middle Ages and used to build the European lute which descended from the 'ûd.[145]

The application of this design in Turkey, in particular since 1950, made it possible to use thinner wood being, moreover, less labour-intensive compared to the carving-hollowing-out of the *oyma* bowl. In contrast to *oyma*, however, a carvel-build bowl (*yaprakli*) is less resistant to moisture. Today, this type of construction is the most common way of construction. Carvel-built bowls are in general amazingly light compared with carved-hollowed-out bowls, but are susceptible to damp and in a humid climate the ribs may split.

Although the instruments vary in size, there is little variation in the thickness of the ribs (around 4 mm). A bowl constructed from ribs is lighter than an *oyma* bowl due to its composition of thin ribs. Mulberry (*dut*), juniper (*ardıç ağacı*), mahogany (*maun ağacı*) and hornbeam (*gürgen ağacı*) are used to make a bowl composed of ribs (*yaprakli*). The bowl is composed of an odd number of ribs (*dilimli*). It is built from a central rib around a wooden or iron mold (*tekne kalıbı*). The ribs are placed in the water for one hour before use. They are then bent with a heated tool or with a bending iron or oven. One by one, the ribs are glued on the front side of the hardwood heel block (*sap dibi takozu, bağlantı takozu, tekne dili*) and on the rear side on the also of hardwood made tail block or inner diadem (*tekne dili, bağlantı takozu*) and temporarily nailed. A strip is often nailed onto the tail block for reinforcement during drying. It is very important for the condition and lifespan of the instrument that the ribs fit well together.

---

[145] Turnbull, H. The Genesis of Carvel-Built Lutes: 79.

The mold is removed two hours after the bowl was made. Glue is now applied on the inside along the joints. For reinforcement, a thin strip of paper or parchment was laid on the inside or outside of the bowl, after which the joints are forged together with a heated tool. After drying, the nails and paper strips are removed. Nowadays, almost no one uses paper strips inside anymore with exception of the 'ûd and Ottoman tanbûr. Ribs of 4 mm have enough surface area for the glue. The paper strip used outside acts as a clamp after applying the glue. The hot iron dries the glue instantly and the paper strip keeps the joint tight.

A sound hole is cut into the tail block into which a rosette is glued as finishing touch. In the yaprakli construction method, the string holder is glued to the tail block between the ribs and finished with a strip of wood. Some luthiers, however, glue the tailpiece in the same way as on a carved bowl.

Other materials, such as metal or horn, are also used for the tailpiece. The joint on the tail block is finished with a wooden strip. Like the oyma bowl, the yaprakli bowl has a V-shaped joint in the heel into which the neck is glued. Süleyman Aslan, however, believes that the neck of the bağlama should not be glued in a V-shaped, but rectangular-shaped joint, although some luthiers see no advantage in a rectangular joint.

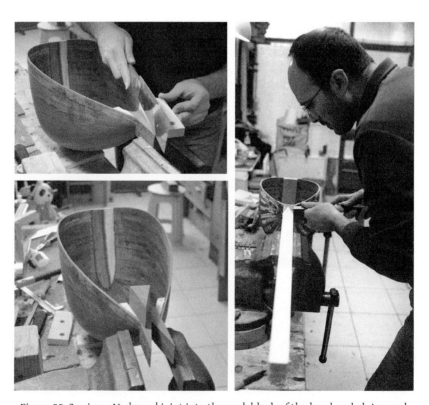

Figure 55. Sawing a V-shaped joint into the neck block of the bowl and gluing and finishing the neck by Engin Topuzkanamış.
© Courtesy Engin Topuzkanımış, Izmir.

Neck and Pegbox

The neck is made of hardwood. The V-shaped ends of the neck are glued into a V-shaped joint in the pegbox and heel or heel block of the bowl. It is believed that a glued neck provides a better resonance as a connection between neck and bowl. The resonance is furthermore determined by the mass or density of the wood and the material used for the bridge and the nut. The neck may be a solid piece of wood or a fretboard may be glued on. The back of the neck is round so that he can easily move his left hand up and down along the neck.

To prevent warping due to the tension of the strings, the neck is shaped like a bow, so that when the strings are tuned the string traction is absorbed by the neck. Moreover, the soundboard continues a few centimetres on the neck. On many contemporary instruments, however, it is not the soundboard, but the glued-on fingerboard that runs over the junction of the neck and bowl to prevent warping.

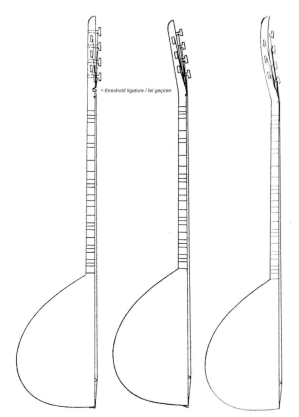

> < threshold ligature / tel geçiren

To ensure that the neck does not warp, some luthiers also install a pull rod in a recess just below the finger board. A similar development took place earlier in America with the introduction of steel strings on the acoustic guitar. A 'pull rod' prevents warping of the neck and a bracing system, small pieces of wood glued underside of the soundboard, neutralize the tension of the steel strings through the bridge on the soundboard.

At the junction of the neck and the pegbox, the of ebony (*abanoz ağacı*) or boxwood (*şimşir*) made nut (*üst eşik*) is placed in a groove. Traditional long-necked lutes had a straight peghead. A 'threshold ligature' (*eşik bağı, tel geçiren*) therefore guarded the strings on the peg side of the nut.[146]

Figure 56. In the past, the neck was generally straight with a 'threshold ligature' (*tel geçiren*) to secure the strings. Instruments with a straight neck are still built (1). In 1950, the luthier Yusuf Atasoy from Ankara introduced an angled pegbox (2). The angled pegbox has become an common feature, some luthiers also make curved ones (3).
© Courtesy Cafer Açın, Istanbul.

The pegbox is also made of hardwood and is glued at a small angle to the neck. If the fingerboard consist of a thin wooden strip, a wooden strip is also glued on the pegbox. Seven tapered holes are drilled in the

---

[146] Picken, L. Folk Musical Instruments of Turkey: 224.

pegbox. The T-shaped tuning pegs are made of hardwood. A small hole is drilled in the top of the pegbox through which a nylon wire is looped enabling the instrument to be hanged on a nail in the wall, a common habit in Turkey.

Tuning the instrument with the wooden tuning pegs is, despite the use of the appropriate timbres, often difficult. Tuning mechanisms such as those of the guitar or mechanisms specially designed for the *bağlama* are also used today. Some players believe that wooden tuning pegs give a better tone than a tuning mechanism. Others feel that a tuning mechanism, although usually heavier than the wooden ones, does not have an audible influence on the tone.

Soundboard

The soundboard (or top) is without doubt the most important piece influencing the sound of an instrument. A soundboard made of a knot-free and well-seasoned thin sheet of soft wood (the thinner the better), preferably spruce or cedar with a straight wire from a high altitude and poor soil, combines the necessary stiffness, lightness, and ability to transmit the soundwaves efficiently. Like the bowl, the soundboard varies in thickness being thicker near the junction of the neck and the bowl, from the bridge to the rim of the bowl, and the edges. As each soundboard has its own natural resonances, it is often tested by ear by tapping on the soundboard or bowing it on the edge to get an idea of how it will respond on the completed instrument.

Usually *bağlama* makers don't use quarter-sawn wood for the soundboard, because they think it's too stiff for a *bağlama*. Instead they prefer rift-sawn wood which has a very straight grain pattern, 60-70 degrees to the face of the board while quarter-sawn wood has 90 degrees. Quarter-sawn and rift-sawn refer to the way in which the trunk has been sawn into planks, namely through and parallel to the axis of the trunk. In the case of pure quarter and rift-sawn wood, the growth rings are primarily visible in the width as stripes and warping does not occur. With slab-sawn wood, warping occurs due to the difference in shrinkage of the different grain directions.

Previously, an arched soundboard (*bombe*), obtained by means of heating, was preferred because of its arched shape it collapsed less quickly. Moreover, the soundboard could be kept thin, which benefits the sound. To prevent tearing, the soundboard was, moreover, not made of one sheet of wood but composed of different sized and coloured wooden panels on either sides of the soundboard called *cheek* (*yanak, yanaklı sazı*).

Most lutes in the countryside of Anatolia had a flat and single soundboard made of soft pine wood. Some rural luthiers also made instruments with a slightly arched single soundboard. The composite and arched soundboard was apparently generally an urban construction method design.[147]

A slightly curved one-piece soundboard is preferred since the second half of the last century, because it produces a more powerful and fuller timbre than a curved and/or composite soundboard. To prevent it from collapsing through the traction of the strings it had, however, to be kept relatively thick. Nevertheless, it still collapses sooner or later.

---

[147] Picken, L. Folk Musical Instruments of Turkey: 214.

The soundboard of the *bağlamas* produced by Kemal Eroğlu is slightly arched at the height of the bridge (*eşik noktası*). Eroğlu also uses mahogany (*maun ağacı, mahunya ağacı*) for the soundboard, spruce (*ladin ağacı*) for the bowl, hornbeam (*gürgen ağacı*) for the neck, for the boxwood for the pegbox, ebony for the bridge, and maple for the nut.

The Turkish luthier Süleyman Aslan is of the opinion that a *bağlama* with a flat soundboard and thin bowl is no longer suitable for the requirements imposed on these instruments since 1960. The heavier stringing is the core of the problem. A flat soundboard collapses eventually when the wood loses its tension due to the string traction. In order to prevent this, he developed a barring system for the *bağlama* searching for a compromise between stiffness and freedom of the soundboard to vibrate properly. An additional advantage was that the soundboard could be kept thin. According to the luthier Engin Topuzkanamış, however, *bağlamas* don't need a bracing system to neutralize the string tension when one uses slightly arched soundboards. The soundboard of *bağlamas* built by Kemal Eroğlu are for the same reason slightly arched at the position of the movable bridge.[148]

The soundboard with sound hole of the by Süleyman Aslan made *Dinç sazı* is supported by a bracing system and a rod was installed in the neck, like the guitar. Although bracing and installing a rod in the neck is a good concept for this instrument, it does not suit a traditional sounding *bağlama*. Carbon fibre rods, which are quite strong and light in weight, are suggested by Engin Topuzkanamış as a possible alternative. The collapsing of the soundboard can also be overcome by using an arched soundboard.[149]

The earliest source about the use of a barring system (Arabic *tastânâ, tastânât*) is the *Hâwî al-funûn wa-salwat al-mahzûn* (Compendium of a Fatimid Court Musician, Cairo, 11th century) of Ibn at-Tahhân al-Mûsîqî, a court musician at the Fatimid court.[150] A soundboard needs in general to be reinforced to increase its rigidity and assure that the vibrations will spread efficiently over the soundboard. Therefore, reinforcement is placed directly under the bridge in the form of a rectangular-shaped strap of wood or a barring system under the soundboard to transport the vibration of the strings via the bridge to the other parts of the soundboard.[151]

The soundboard is glued on the rim of the bowl. The instrument is then varnished to protect it from scratches, bumps, sweat, and dirt. Varnish is applied with a brush or with a syringe. Modern spray varnishes, such as polyurethane are extremely hard, unlike polish, and therefore offer good protection, although they influence the timbre. A number of synthetic varnishes are not suitable for acoustic instruments, because they can affect the sound negatively. The composition of a varnish, as well as the way in which and to what degree it is applied (not too thick and too hard), affects the sound quality.

---

[148] Engin Topuzkanamış. Personal communication; Kemal Eroğlu. Personal communication.
[149] Engin Topuzkanamış. Personal communication.
[150] Neubauer, E. Der Bau der Laute und ihre Besaitigung nach Arabischen, Persischen und Türkischen Quellen des 9. bis 15. Jahrhunderts: 301-302.
[151] Hopkin, B. Musical Instrument Design: Practical Information for Instrument Making: 107, 110.

Frets, Bridge, and Strings

The frets (*bağı, perde* or *perde bağı*) were originally made from sheep-gut (*koyun barsağı* or *koyun kirişi*) or copper wire (*bakır perdeli*). Nylon thread (fishing line, 0.3-0.6 mm) has been used for the frets since around forty years. The nylon frets are wrapped around the neck a number of times and not tied too tightly, so that they can be easily be shifted to change their tuning. To facilitate the tying of the frets, a channel (*oluk*) was carved in the past in the left side of the neck.

The frets are placed on the neck and tied as follows: halfway between the bridge and the comb the fret of the octave lies on the open string, one third of that of the fifth and one quarter of this the quarter fret. The remaining frets are placed by ear.

The strings rest on a flat triangular-shaped and movable bridge (*alt eşik*), which is held in place by the pressure of the strings. The height of the bridge determines the tone quality, tone colour, and the damping of the strummed or plucked strings. With a given set of strings and tunings, the lower the bridge, the better the response of the soundboard and the bowl to higher frequencies in the sound of the strings. [152]

The bridge is made of maple wood (*akça ağaç, maple ağacı* or *kelebek ağacı*) and is located on the soundboard above the deepest point of the bowl. The height of the bridge partly determines the tonal quality and depends on the size of the instrument (4-7.5 mm). Süleyman Aslan also builds instruments of which the bridge is mounted on the top like the guitar, made possible by the barring system under the soundboard.

In the West, gut strings were already known in antiquity. In the Far East, the use of silk strings has been around for centuries. Metal strings were known in China in the 14th century, possibly even since the 9th century during the Tang period. Metal strings were manufactured in Europe from the fourteenth century, when they were needed for keyboard instruments such as the clavichord, the spinet, the harpsichord, and the virginal. At a later stage, strings were wound with copper, silver, steel or aluminium wire to increase the mass and thus the volume.

Strings made of sheep gut are mentioned by Yûnus Emre's. In the 17th century Turkish long-necked lutes still had gut strings. According to Evliyâ Çelebi, the first mentioned lute having metal strings is the *tel tanbûr* from Kütahya (West Anatolia, 17th century). In the 18th and 19th centuries, the *saz* was strung with metal strings from Venice. [153] Stringing Turkish long-necked lutes with metal strings was probably an urban feature and more specific of stringed instruments of Ottoman classical music. Rural long-necked lutes were strung with gut strings into the 20th century.

The two strings of the *tanbûr* were initially expanded with a third one. More strings were added in the course of time, to amplify the sound volume and enrich the tone, grouped in single, double or triple courses (2:1, 2:2, 3:2, 3:2:2, 3:3:3, 3:3:1).

---

[152] Picken, L. Folk Musical Instruments of Turkey: 212, 214.
[153] Picken, L. Folk Musical Instruments of Turkey: 269-270.

In the Persian musical tradition, the term *tanbûr* is alternatingly used with names specifying the number of strings, i.e. *dutâr* for a two-stringed lute and *setâr* for a three-stringed lute. In Anatolia this was initially also the case: '*iki telli*' for a two-stringed and '*üç telli*' for a three-stringed lute. Folk musicians used to speak of 'oniki tell' for a twelve-stringed *saz*, '*on telli*' for a ten-stringed *saz* (3+4+3), '*yedi telli*' for a seven-stringed *saz* (3+2+2) and '*altı telli*' for a six-stringed *saz* (2+2+2). The habit of naming lutes by their number of strings has apparently not yet completely been abandoned, like *dört telli bağlama* for a four-course *bağlama* (2+2+2+2) and *üç telli* for a three-stringed instrument.[154]

The first string course of the contemporary *bağlama* consists of two steel strings and a wound string. The middle course (*orta teller*) consists of two steel strings and the third course (*üst teller*) consists of a steel string and a wound string. The material used for wrapping consists of silver-coloured stainless steel, nickel, nickel alloy, gold-coloured bronze, copper, silver-plated copper or other alloys. The number and type of strings can be changed according to the playing technique and personal preferences. In the *şelpe* playing technique one string is used for each course.

A standard set for the long-necked *bağlama* consists of two steel strings of 0.20 mm and an octave string of 0.42 mm for the first course, two steel strings of 0.30 for the middle course, and for the third course a steel string of 0.20 mm and an octave string of 0.52 mm. A standard set on the short-necked *bağlama* consists of two steel strings of 0.18 mm and an octave string of 0.40 mm for the first course, two steel strings of 0.28 mm for the middle course, and one steel string of 0.18 mm and an octave string of 0.50 mm for the third course.[155]

Ornamentation

In Turkey, in contrast to Central Asia, there was in general no tradition until 1950 to apply ornamentations (*süsleme*) to musical instruments. An exception to this were the instruments built by Armenians and Greeks in the second half of the 19th century and the first half of the 20th century. In the past, however, a client wanted to show his social status by means of ornamentations in the form of marquetry of gold, precious stones, mother-of-pearl, ivory. In general, however, luthiers and musicians believe that the fine-tuning and appearance of instruments have an adverse effect on the sound.

A furthermore exception are the incised burned designs of the bowls and soundboards of Gaziantep, being a long time feature of the *sazs* from Gaziantep. From the Gaziantep region, also inlay patterns on the front of the neck, executed in mother-of-pearl and pear or apple-wood. In the past, instrument makers sometimes applied symbolic ornamentations which, however, did not have the same symbolic meaning as the motifs on carpets and kilims. They probably had a personal character. The master luthier Hüseyin Tavşancı once built a *bağlama* with an image of the mystic Hacı Bektaş Veli (1209-1271) on the soundboard.[156]

---

[154] Feldman, W. Music of the Ottoman Court. Makam, Composition and the Early Ottoman Instrumental Repertoire: 143; Picken, L. Folk Musical Instruments of Turkey: 210.
[155] Engin Topuzkanamış. Personal communication.
[156] Picken, L. Folk Musical Instruments of Turkey: 278-279.

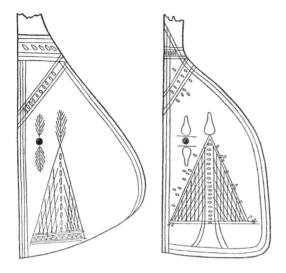

Figure 57. Traditional Incised burned designs in bowls from Ganziantep.
© Courtesy Oxford University Press, Oxford.

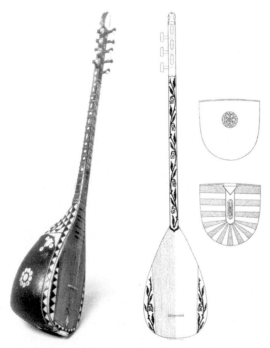

Figure 58. Turkish *saz* with inlay of mother-of-pearl from the Ottoman court (19th century, left). Ornamentation designs by Cafer Açın (right).
© Kulsan Foundation, Amsterdam / Topkapı Sarayı Müzesi, Istanbul. 8/845.
© Courtesy Cafer Açın, Istanbul.

After 1950, decorative motifs were increasingly used in instrument construction, usually in the form of simple geometric figures (circles, stars, triangles, or diamonds) or stylized motifs from flora and fauna (trees, flowers, birds). This was done in the form of wood carvings and inlays on the bowl, soundboard, and neck. Various types of wood (*farklı ağaç türleri*), mother-of-pearl (*sedef*), ivory (*fildişi*), bone (*kemik*), tortoise-shell (*kaplumbağa*), pear or apple-wood and in particular cases precious stones were used.

Since the second half of the last century, the bowl has been partially veneered (*kaplamak*), the neck and pegbox completely veneered with a hard type of wood. *Yapraklı* in particular lends itself well to decorating the bowl, because the veneered parts can be combined with the ribs. Geometric motifs can also be applied to the veneered parts. In addition, the *yapraklı* can be composes of alternating dark and light strips. The strip between the ribs on the tailpiece also offers decorative options.

Two areas of the *bağlama* in particular permit elaborate ornamentation. The upper end of the neck and the sound hole(s). A composite soundboard offers, moreover, also decorative possibilities by composing the soundboard of three or more panels of different in colour varying types of wood. A artfully carved rosette carved is often glued into the sound hole and the top of the neck was often also artfully carved into a small and decorative knob. A tassel (*püskül*) is still attached to the top of the neck.

See YouTube for the construction of *bağlamas* as well as *Oğur sazıs*.

Chapter-4
Tuning

Over the centuries there have been many tunings determining the number and tuning of frets and strings. They vary largely depending on the musical tradition and changing musical and tonal demands made on them. Fret and string tunings in Turkey varied, like the long-necked lutes, regionally as well as locally. Whereas some early folk lutes have frets tuned according to a diatonic scale, the older Anatolian string tunings were in general the same as those of Central Asia (in fourth or fifths). Nowadays, most Turkish long-necked lutes have chromatically tuned frets in a non-equal tempered scale, while two important tunings (*düzenlemek* from *düzen* meaning ordering, arranging) became standard, the *bozuk düzeni* or *kara düzen* and the *bağlama düzeni* or *âşık düzeni*.[157]

String Tuning

After the standardization of Turkish folk music, the *bozuk düzeni* or *kara düzen* (I:aaA, II:dd, III:gG) for the long-necked *bağlama* and the *bağlama düzeni* or *âşık düzeni* (I:ddD, II:gg, III:aA) for the short-necked *bağlama* became ultimately standard. This tuning, applied by Arif Sağ to the short-necked *bağlama*, became in a short time very popular in the 1980s and is therefore sometimes also called *Arif düzeni*. The lower string group, the first course, is the highest sounding course. The upper string of the first and third string groups, the so-called octave strings, are tuned one octave lower (indicated by a capital letter). Some musicians also replace the upper string of the middle string group with an octave string.

On a *bağlama* tuned in *bozuk düzeni*, the a-course is primarily played as melody course, the d and g-courses are the mainly open (not with the left hand played) bourdon courses. In principle, the location of a piece is chosen such that d or g is the final note (*karar sesi* or *karar perdesi*). This can then be enhanced by the open d or g-courses. Rarely is a piece organized in such a way that a is the final note. After all, in that case there is no second single string that can strengthen the closing note. However, if this is the case for some reason, there are two possibilities to obtain the desired reinforcement of the closing note by a second string. The first is to shorten the g-course with the thumb on the third fret to a at the end. This practice is mainly found in Kırşehir and Keskin (Central Anatolia) and is called *abdal düzeni*. The second is by pre-tuning the g-course or d-course to a in advance. In that case, one speaks of *kayseri düzeni*. Similar tunings are also applied to the short-necked *bağlama* tuned in *bağlama düzeni*.

Another important point regarding the string tuning are the intervals between the courses. In the *bağlama düzeni*, for example, the interval between the first and second courses is a quarter and between the second and third courses a large second. The larger *tanbura* is tuned a quarter lower in *bağlama düzeni*: I:aaA, II:dd, III:eE.

In some parts of Anatolia, different tunings are still in circulation. The most important of these are the *misket düzeni* (I:aaA, II:dd, III:fisFis) and the *müstezat düzeni* or *karanfil düzeni* (I:aaA, II:dd,

---

[157] See Picken, L. Folk Musical Instruments of Turkey: 284, 285-288; During, J. and J. Baily. Tanbûr: 61.

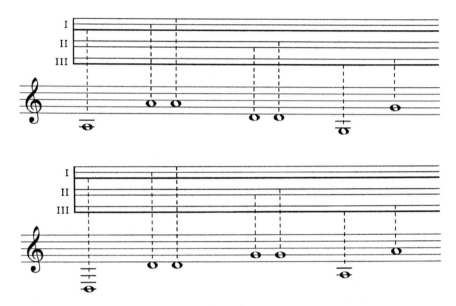

Figure 59. *Bozuk düzeni* or *kara düzeni* (above). *Bağlama düzeni* or *âşık düzeni* (below).
© Author.

III:fF), a characteristic local tuning for *tanburas*. The use of these tunings has become quite rare.

The *bozlak* songs in Central Anatolia are played in the *bozlak düzeni* or *abdal düzeni* (I:aaA, II:aa, III:gG). The *hüdayda* and *füdayda* melodies from Ankara are played in the *hüdayda düzeni* (I:aaA, II:dd, III:dD), with the melody being performed on the middle course. The strings of the middle and third courses are then plucked in a sweeping movement of the plectrum.

The last tuning to be mentioned here is the *ırızva* or *kara düzeni* (I:aaA, II:dd, III:aA), which is used for the *ırızva*, a small *saz*, by the Alevî and Bektaşî dedes during their religious gatherings. According to Kemal Eroğlu, who is still building the *ırızva*, the profile of this small *saz* with its conical-shaped bowl resembles the crane (*turna*), the holy bird of the Alevî. There is a sound hole on the right side of the bowl. The *ırızva* played by the Alevî dedes has three soundholes on the right side of the bowl, symbolizing respectively Allah, the Prophet, and Ali.

Fret Tuning

Another significant development after the standardization of folk music was the effort to standardize the number and tuning of frets on the Turkish long-necked lutes. Until this time, the number of frets and their tuning varied on the traditional long-necked lutes. For centuries the fret tuning was either tempered or contained more or less indefinite microtones. The expansion of the frets with microtones was the work of Muzaffer Sarısözen. The total number of frets, which was previously generally 6, 7, 10, 12, and 17, increased in a short time to 25, 30, and finally even up to 50.

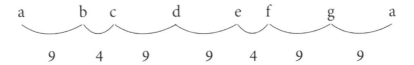

Figure 60. Diatonic scale and distance between the commas.
© Author.

Long-necked lutes had initially no microtonal frets according to the *bağlama* players Orhan Dağli (*d.* 2012) and Ali Ekber Çiçek (1935-2006), and the singer Neriman Tüfekci (1926-2009). The number of frets were, according to Adnan Ataman, increasingly expanded under the influence of urban folk music and Ottoman classical music. The expansion of the number of frets with microtonal frets were, however, interpreted and criticized in various ways.[158]

In Turkish music theory, the size of a pitch is expressed in so-called commas. A comma is one-ninth part of a whole tone according to the diatonic tuning. In a diatonic tuning, a whole tone includes nine commas, a semitone four. An octave therefore consists of fifty-three commas.

Each of these tones has a separate fret on the *bağlama*. In addition, there are five frets for the chromatic notes, Bes, Cis, Es, Fis and As, each of which is five commas higher than the adjacent diatonic tone. Finally, there are five more frets for the non-chromatic tones B-, C +, E-, F + and A-. As a standard, a contemporary *bağlama* has seventeen frets in an octave. The range of a string is, as shown on the right, a duodecime (octave plus a fifth), meaning that there are twenty-four frets on the neck of the *bağlama*.

Countryside

The difference between the rural lutes and those in the city is the number of frets and their location on the neck. Lutes in the countryside generally had fewer frets than those in the city: seven to twelve frets compared to fourteen to nineteen frets. The tuning of frets on Turkish long-necked lutes did not only differ per region, but also from city to city and even from village to village. The *bağlamas* in south-eastern Turkey are, in contrast to those of Central Anatolia, characterized by more frets, including frets for non-diatonic pitch intervals. The same applies to the *bağlamas* of the *âşıks* from Kars (north-eastern Anatolia).

The way in which the tuning of the frets on the long-necked lutes of the countryside was determined goes back to the 13th and possibly even 9th century. On the countryside, the frets were not tuned in a fully chromatic tuning. In addition, there existed the simple, diatonic tuning of the frets, which was similar to that of Central Asia.

The tuning of frets on rural *bağlamas* is currently generally in line with that of the city. The number of frets has approximately a range of one and a half octaves per string or course. In the past the number of frets was sometimes extended on the soundboard with glued-on reed

---

[158] Parlak, E. Standardization of the bağlama and the development of its notation from the founding of the republic to the present, in Çiftçi, N. and M. Greve (eds) Die Bağlama in der Türkei und Europa. Erstes Bağlama-Symposium in Deutschland. Berlin, 14-15 September 2013: 95-98; See also Stokes, M. The Arabesk Debate. Music and Musicians in Modern Turkey: 50-88.

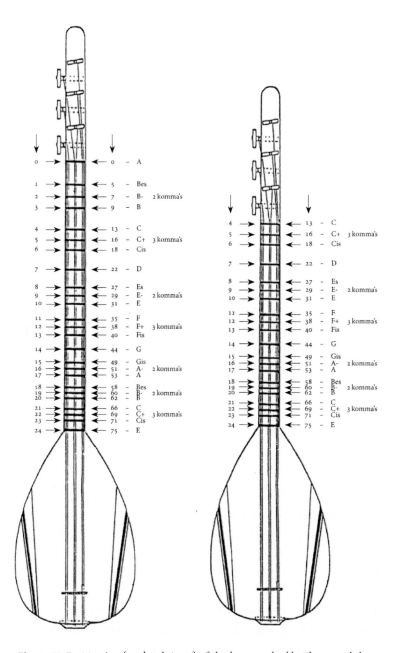

Figure 61. Fret tuning (*perde taksimati*) of the long-necked bağlama and the
short-necked bağlama according to Cafer Açın.
© Cafer Açın / Author, Istanbul.

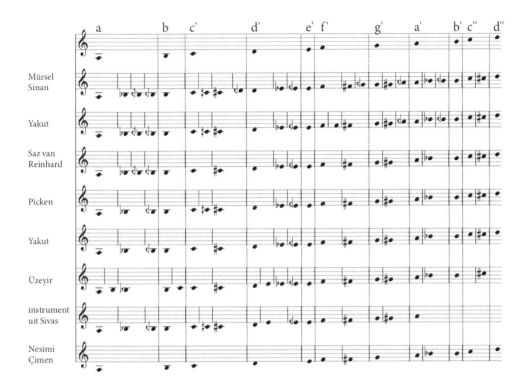

Figure 62. Various number of frets and their tuning.
© Courtesy Dietrich Reimer Verlag.

frets (*kamış perdeleri*). Frets glued on the soundboard can also be found on other instruments of the *tanbûr* family.

City

Lutes in the city had fourteen to nineteen frets in the past. The contemporary long-necked *bağlama* has twenty-four frets, that is, a range of an octave and a quarter per string or course. The short-necked *bağlama* has twenty frets, that is, a range of one octave and one second per string or course.

Around 1940 there was increasing standardization of the number of frets and their tuning, a development in which besides Muzaffer Sarısözen, Mahmut Ragıp Gazimihâl (1900-1961) also played an important role. This development took place around Radio Ankara and aimed at reforming the music and musical instruments of the many regions, each with their own characteristics, into a coherent whole. To that end, choirs and orchestras were set up to perform uniform folk music on standardized lutes, from 1938 for Radio Ankara and after 1950 also for Radio Istanbul by Sâdi Yâver Ataman (1906-1994) with his own music company and the *Yurttan Sesler Topluluğu* ('Sounds of our country ') in cooperation with Muzaffer Sarısözen. The current choirs and orchestras of the TRT are a reflection of that of Ottoman classical music.

La	Si♭	**Si♭³**	**Si♭²**	Si	Do	**Do♯** **Do♭**	Re	Mi♭	**Mi♭³**	**Mi♭²**	Mi	Fa	Fa♯ Sol♭	Sol	La♭	**La♭²**	La

Figure 63. The distribution of frets in the octave by Muzaffer Sarısözen. In *Yurttan Sesler*, Sarısözen indicated the comma value in the octave by means of a number at the note on the staff. The bold notes are non-chromatic. Calculated from the bridge (fret 0) there are seventeen frets in the octave. Five of them are non-chromatic frets (up). Muzaffer Sarısözen and the *Yurttan Sesler Topluluğu* in Ankara, 1950s (left).
© Author.
© Unknown source.

The *bağlama* plays a central role, supplemented by instruments such as *kemence, kanun, târ, 'ûd,* guitar, bass guitar, and drums.[159]

The number of frets increased rapidly in a short time, rising to twenty-five, thirty, and even fifty frets. It is therefore not surprising that musicians initially had difficulty with the increasing number of frets: 'bu saz radyo *sazı*, ben çala-mam' ('this *saz* is a radio *saz*, I can't play on that'). In 1952, Sarısözen started to indicate the comma value by means of a number on the note on the *staff*, a practice that was, although also criticized, generally accepted. He was also one of the first to choose to fret the *bağlama* with seventeen frets in the octave.

Around 1970 there was still a great variety in the number of frets and their tuning. In 1971, for example, Şemsi Yastıman (1923-1994), a well-known urban *âşık* born in Kırşehir, played a *bağlama* with fifteen frets in the octave. Yastıman played an important role in the reform of Turkish folk music in general and in the development of traditional and informal music education handed down from father to son into a formal and institutionalized education at music schools and conservatories in particular.[160]

Nail Tan (1941) concluded in *Bağlama yapımı* that in general seventeen frets were used for the octave, but that the number of frets and their tuning of non-chromatic frets was not yet standardized. In the second half of the 1980s, there seems to be some consensus. Sabri Yener in *Bağlama Öğretim Metodu* and Irfan Kurt in *Bağlamada düzen ve pozisyon* both established seventeen frets in the octave, including five non-chromatic frets. Cafer Açın established in *Bağlama. Yapım sanatı ve sanatçıları* seventeen frets in the octave for the long-necked as well as the short-necked *bağlama*.

The number of frets and tuning of non-diatonic frets can be adjusted if the player wishes. Some players, such as the late Neşet Ertaş, added extra non-chromatic frets (microtonal frets) to their *bağlamas* as a demonstration of their virtuosity.

---

[159] See for discussion Parlak, E. Standardisierung der Bağlama und die Entwicklung ihrer Notation von der Republiksgründung bis zur Gegenwart, in in Çiftçi, N. and M. Greve (eds) Die Bağlama in der Türkei und Europa. Erstes Bağlama-Symposium in Deutschland. Berlin, 14-15 September 2013.
[160] See for further discussion Section IV Das Studium der Bağlama, in Çiftçi, N. and M. Greve (eds) Die Bağlama in der Türkei und Europa. Erstes Bağlama-Symposium in Deutschland. Berlin, 14-15 September 2013: 261-316.

Figure 64. Muzafer Sarısözen and Şemsi Yastıman both playing a large *saz* of which the frets extend on the soundboard.
© Unknown source.

0	1	2	3	4	5	6	7	8	9	10	11	12	13	14	15	16	17
La	Si$_b$	**Si$_b^2$**	Si	Do	**Do$_\#^3$**	Do$_\#$	Re	Mi$_b$	**Mi$_b^2$**	Mi	Fa	**Fa$_\#^3$**	Fa$_\#$	Sol	La$_b$	**La$_b^2$**	La

0	1	2	3	4	5	6	7	8	9	10	11	12	13	14	15	16	17
Re	Mi$_b$	**Mi$_b^2$**	Mi	Fa	**Fa$_\#^3$**	Fa$_\#$	Sol	La$_b$	**La$_b^2$**	La	Si$_b$	**Si$_b^2$**	Si	Do	**Do$_\#^3$**	Do$_\#$	Re
	La$_b$	**La$_b^2$**	La	Si$_b$	**Si$_b^2$**	Si	Do										
	Si$_b$	**Si$_b^2$**	Si	Do	**Do$_\#^3$**	Do$_\#$	Re										

Figure 65. Contemporary fret tuning of the octave of the long-necked *bağlama* and the short-necked *bağlama*. The bold notes are non-chromatic. Calculated from the bridge (ferret 0) there are seventeen ferrets in the octave of the long-necked *bağlama* and short-necked *bağlama*. Five of them are non-chromatic frets.
© Author.

Figure 66. Neşet Ertaş playing a *saz* with an amazingly large oval-shaped bowl and a large number of frets.
© Courtesy Ulaş Özdemir, Istanbul.

According to instrument builder Süleyman Aslan, the small *bağlamas* of rural Anatolia did not only have a limited number of frets, but also no more than three single strings, strummed with the fingers until the second half of the last century. They became marginalized after the establishment of the Republic of Turkey and *bağlamas* with a larger number of frets and doubled or tripled-stringed courses plucked with a plectrum were introduced.[161]

---

[161] Süleyman Aslan. Personal Communication.

Chapter-5
Playing Technique

In the past there were significant differences between the playing styles of urban and rural musicians which have largely levelled out in the meantime. The *bağlama* proper, with a bowl length of 45-46 cm and tuned according to the widespread *bozuk düzeni*, was for a long time standard among famous musicians, at the radio, and music market as well. The *bağlama* player Bayram Aracı (1925-1985) played an important role In the development and passing on of the playing technique of this *bağlama* tuned in *bozuk düzeni*, an influence which continues up till today among professionals as well as non-professionals. Davut Sulari (1925-1985), influenced by Bayram Aracı, introduced the playing technique of this *bağlama* tuned in *bozuk düzeni* in the Alevî musical tradition. One of his students was Ali Ekber Çiçek. The by Bayram Aracı established playing technique and tuning reached its zenith with Neşet Ertaş.[162]

Under influence of Neşet Ertaş, the playing technique of this *bağlama* type tuned in *bozuk düzeni* remained popular and was even called *Neşetkâr* (Neşet's Instrument). The name felled into oblivion when he lived in Germany for several years. In his absence, the instrument became known as the 45'lik *bağlama*, referring to the length of the bowl. After his return to Turkey this *bağlama* type and playing technique became popular again among a younger generation, calling his instrument *abdal sazı* and its tuning *abdal düzeni* or, later, *bozlak düzeni*.[163]

The introduction of the short-necked *bağlama* in the 1980s and its following popularity interrupted the development of the *bağlama* family. The potential possibilities of the long-necked lutes of the *bağlama* family should once again be brought into the spotlight and given priority. The *bağlama* family should, according to Erol Parlak, furthermore be expanded and taught on the basis of the two basic playing techniques, the plectrum technique and the *şelpe* finger technique using the 45'lik *bağlama*.[164]

Playing Position

The bowl is placed on the right upper leg by the seated player in such a way that the soundboard and fingerboard are parallel to his upper body. The soundboard and fingerboard, and therefore also the strings, are not visible to him. A movement from the lower to the higher notes is in the Turkish concept a downward movement (*aşağı*) and from the higher to the lower notes an upward movement (*yukarı*) along the neck.

---

[162] Parlak, E. Standardisierung der Bağlama und die Entwicklung ihrer Notation von der Republiksgründung bis zur Gegenwart, in Çiftçi, N. and M. Greve (eds) Die Bağlama in der Türkei und Europa. Erstes Bağlama-Symposium in Deutschland. Berlin, 14-15 September 2013: 91-92.

[163] Parlak, E. Standardisierung der Bağlama und die Entwicklung ihrer Notation von der Republiksgründung bis zur Gegenwart, in Çiftçi, N. and M. Greve (eds) Die Bağlama in der Türkei und Europa. Erstes Bağlama-Symposium in Deutschland. Berlin, 14-15 September 2013: 91-92.

[164] Parlak, E. Standardization of the bağlama and the development of its notation from the founding of the republic to the present, in Çiftçi, N. and M. Greve (eds) Die Bağlama in der Türkei und Europa. Erstes Bağlama-Symposium in Deutschland. Berlin, 14-15 September 2013: 98-99.

The neck rests on the palm between the thumb and forefinger, keeping the wrist slightly bent. In this way the thumb can be bent over the edge of the fingerboard to shorten the third course. The right forearm, which rests on the curve of the bowl, holds the instrument in balance, with the neck of the instrument pointing slightly upwards. The instrument does not rest on the player's left hand in any way. With the fingers of the right hand or a plectrum, the strings are played halfway between the bridge and the fretboard. Close to the bridge the strings timbre sharp or metallic, towards the middle and further the timbre becomes softer and fuller.

Finger Positions

For a good understanding of the fingering, the numbering of the fingers of the left hand is important. The index finger (*işaret parmağı*) is number one, the middle finger (*orta parmak*) two, the ring finger (*yüzük parmağı*) three, the little finger (*küçük parmak*) four, and the thumb (*baş parmak*) number five. The thumb is kept free to shorten the third course.

The fingering is determined by the following principles. An entire tone is played with the first and third fingers. Bigger jumps with the first and fourth finger or simply by sliding the hand up and using the first, second or third finger. Smaller distances are played with the first and second fingers. The index finger performs most of the work and is supported by the other fingers and thumb. A figuration typical of the *bağlama* is the *çarpma*, in which the string is hammered several times quickly by the second or third finger. This can be further accentuated by means of separate pick movements. The *çarpma* is often decorated by pulling down and releasing the played string course.

There is some discussion about the use of the little finger. Some musicians believe that the use of the little finger is inevitable if one wants to minimize the sliding of the index finger. Older musicians often stick to avoiding the use of the little finger. They think the little finger is too weak to function independently and must therefore always be supported by the third finger. On the short-necked bağlama, however, the use of the little finger in vertical play is unavoidable.[165]

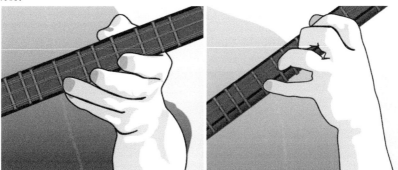

Figure 67. Left hand position of the horizontal playing technique without using the little finger. Left hand position of the vertical playing technique using the little finger.
© Author.

---

[165] Stokes, M. The Arabesk Debate. Music and Musicians in Modern Turkey: 73.

Plectrum Techniques

The use of a plectrum (*tezene*) stems from the Arabic music culture and perhaps goes back to antiquity. The general use of a plectrum and metal strings dates from the early period of the Republic of Turkey (1930s) and resulted in a higher volume and a clear tone. In present-day Turkey, the long-necked lutes are generally plucked with a plectrum. An exception to this are the smaller long-necked lutes and the short-necked *bağlama*, which are also played with the fingers.

Now the *şelpe* finger technique has become more sophisticated, the short-necked *bağlama* seems to be less suitable for this technique. Experiments are therefore conducted with other forms of stringing as well as the shape of the bowl, a drop-shaped bowl suits the *şelpe* playing technique better than a pear-shaped bowl. This seems plausible since the finger-strummed Central Asian lutes also have drop-shaped bowls. *Bağlamas* with a drop-shaped bowl with soundholes, a slightly curved soundboard at the location of the bridge, and steel strings are made by Kemal Eroğlu.

Plectrums were, before they were made of plastic, made of cherry bark (*kiraz ağscının kabuğu*), rounded at one end and square at the other. To prevent this plectrum for drying out it was soaked and kept in olive oil and to prevent warping kept stacked together and bound to a strip of wood giving them a durability of ten years. *Bağlama* players among the Bektaşi dervishes used a plectrum made of water-buffalo (*manda boynuzu*) delivering the necessary sound volume to accompany the secret and sacred rites and dances during their religious ceremonies.[166]

Nâzım Hikmet (1902-1963), probably the most important innovator of Turkish poetry in the 20th century, mentions in *Insan Manzaraları* (Human Landscapes, 1940-1947) the use of a cherry wood plectrum. Plectrums made from cherry tree bark were not very durable. According to Arif Sağ, Şemsi Yastıman made a plastic plectrum for the *bağlama* in 1958 based on the guitar plectrum, which underwent a number of improvements in the meantime.

The plectrum, having an oval shape enabling rapid rhythmic movements, is clamped between the tip of the thumb and the index finger while the middle finger is used to hammer rhythmically on the soundboard (*fiske*). The protruding part can optionally be shortened or extended to vary the flexibility of the spectrum and thus the force with which the strings are plucked. The plectrum is, if not used, clamped behind the bridge between the bowl and the strings.

The plectrum technique, together with the ornamentation, forms the style (*tavır*). Musicians are expected to be familiar with the regional plectrum techniques. In many cases, however, they specialize in the plectrum technique of a certain region. Central Anatolia is the most important region for studying the performance, the *tavır* and the repertory of the *bağlama*. There are eight regional *tavrı* established in the theory of folk music of which the *Zeybek tavrı*, *Konya tavrı*, *Sürmeli tavrı*, *Silifke tavrı*, and *Halay tavrı* are the best known.[167]

---

[166] Picken, L. Folk Musical Instruments of Turkey: 227.
[167] Stokes, M. The Arabesk Debate. Music and Musicians in Modern Turkey: 76-81; Gülâ, C. Bağlamada Tezene Tavırları (CD).

Figure 68. Plectrum between thumb and index finger. The middle finger is used to tap rhythmically on the soundboard (*fiske*).
© Author.

Plectrum notation can generally only be found in teaching methods. There are three basic movements:[168]

- From top to bottom on all three courses.
- Down over the first course.
- Up over the first course.

An accentuated note is played with a downward movement and the other notes with an upward movement of the plectrum. The right hand is moved as little as possible. The speed, flexibility and energy required for the attack are the result of a rotating movement of the arm and wrist. Characteristic of Anatolia is the aforementioned rhythmic hammering on the top with the top of the middle finger (*fiske*). This is slightly bent behind the index finger during playing. Another rhythmic technique is that with the nails of the fingers a rolling, tapping, movement is made on the side of the bowl and the soundboard.

Finger Techniques

Playing the smaller-sized *bağlamas* with the fingers of the right hand is a Central Asian technique that ended up with the Turks in Anatolia. This complex and varied technique is based on the execution of rhythmic patterns, in which thumb and fingers are used in various combinations.

This finger technique, which has a number of regional variations, is called *pençe* or *şelpe*. In Central, East and Southeast Anatolia, these were the names for sliding with the right hand. The word *pençe* from Persian means five and refers to the fingers and thumb of the right hand. For the Alevî and the Bektaşî, *pençe* symbolizes the family of the Prophet (Muhammad, Ali, Ayşe, Hasan, and Hüseyin). *Çertme*, a word from Central Asia, and *şelpe* derived therefrom, both also refer to playing with the fingers of the right hand.

The *şelpe* finger technique includes two forms of 'fret taping': the *parmak vurma tekniği* (hammering, *parmak vurma technique*) and the *tel çekme tekniği* (pulling, *tel çekme technique*).

---

[168] Stokes, M. The Arabesk Debate. Music and Musicians in Modern Turkey: 77.

Both the *şelpe/pençe* playing technique and the associated *parmak vurma* playing technique and *tel çekme* playing technique have been described in detail by Erol Parlak in *El ile bağlama çalma (şelpe) tekniği metodu, I and II*. Parlak not only visited Ramazan Güngör to study the *şelpe* playing technique and *parmak vurma* playing technique, but also travelled to Kyrgyzstan and Kazakhstan to study finger technique and make film recordings. Besides Ramazan Güngör, Arif Sağ, and Hasret Gültekin were important examples for him.[169]

Due to the rise and increasing use of a plectrum in the 1930s, the *şelpe* playing technique faded into the background. Only Yörük Türkmen in the Teke region of Anatolia, the Alevî and the Bektaşî in Central, South and Eastern Anatolia, and to a certain extent the Oğuzeli Türkmen in the Gaziantep region still apply this playing technique. In the 1980s, it was Arif Sağ in particular who applied the *şelpe technique* and the *parmak vurma* playing techniques, originally a simple nomad technique on small lutes, to the short-necked *bağlama*. In the meantime significant progress has been made in the *şelpe* playing technique.

The adaptation and further development of this technique on the short-necked *bağlama* took quite some time. Arif Sağ's former students, Erol Parlak and Erdal Erzincan, continue to develop and enrich the *şelpe* technique with new forms of fret tapping and guitar techniques. In the meantime they have established an amazing virtuosity.

In addition, both published *bağlama* methods teaching the plectrum and/or *şelpe* finger technique. Erol Parlak published in 2001 *El İle Bağlama Çalma (Şelpe) Tekniği Metodu 1* and in 2005 *El İle Bağlama Çalma (Şelpe) Tekniği Metodu 2* and in 2011 a German edition *Erol Parlak Bağlama (Saz) Okulu – Schule – Method. Parmak Tekniği (Şelpe) İçin Sistematik Kılavuz, Cilt 1/Eine systematische Anleitung für die Fingerspieltechnik (Şelpe) Technique*, Vol. 1. In 2009, Erdal Erzincan published together with Arif Sağ *Bağlama Metodu. Bağlama Method. Bağlama Düzeni. Bağlama Tuning. Cilt I ve II. Alıştırmalar ve Repertuvar. Exercise and Repertoire.*

Figure 69. Erdal Erzincan playing *şelpe* and *parmak vurma technique* on the short-necked *bağlama*.
© Author.

Volume I and II. In 2019, Erdal Erzincan published *Bağlama İçin Besteler. Compositions for Bağlama. Bağlama, Bozuk, Misket ve Müstezat Düzenlerinde. In Bağlama, Bozuk, Misket and Müstezat Tunings.* In Germany, Ersoy Özgür published in 2013 *Lehrbuch für Bağlama. Bağlama Method.* These bilingual publications are significant contributions to the improvement of *bağlama* teaching at music schools as well as for studying Turkish music at conservatories in Turkey as well in Europe and beyond.

---

[169] Parlak, E. 2001. El İle Bağlama Çalma (Şelpe) Tekniği Metodu 1; Parlak, E. 2005. El İle Bağlama Çalma (Şelpe) Tekniği Metodu 2;Parlak, E. 2011. Erol Parlak Bağlama (Saz) Okulu – Schule – Method. Parmak Tekniği (Şelpe) İçin Sistematik Kılavuz, Cilt 1/Eine systematische Anleitung für die Fingerspieltechnik (Şelpe) Technique, Vol. 1.

Nowadays, the *bağlama* is not only played with the fingers, but also plucked with the fingernails, a technique introduced by Erkan Oğur on an instrument that he had acquired in 1995 and which he called *kopuz*. Oğur uses the fingernails of the first three fingers, the thumb, and index and middle finger (fingernail technique. The thumb, index and middle fingers are used in different combinations to play arpeggios (playing one note at a time) while the melody is played with the index and middle fingers. Especially, the transition of melodies (to link one section to another) by arpeggios is innovative.[170]

On a six-stringed version of the *Oğur sazı* the fingernail technique is as follows. There can be two tonics, either the 2nd or the 5th string. When you take the 2nd string as tonic the thumbnail usually plays the upper two strings as accompanying lines, while the index or middle finger plays the melody on the 1st and 2nd string. When the 5th string is taken as tonic, the melody is played on the 1st, 2nd, and 5th string. The 3rd and 4th string are usually just for arpeggios and the 5th and 6th string as drone or accompanying strings. Examples of the playing technique on the *Oğur sazı* by musicians such as Efrén López and Gilad Weiss can be found on YouTube.[171]

The *bağlama* player Kemal Dinç (1970) introduced after his classical guitar training various guitar playing techniques on the *bağlama*. While adopting these guitar techniques on the *bağlama*, he came to the conclusion that some adjustments on the *bağlama* had to be made, like the tension of the strings, their tuning etc., resulting in a new sound. The playing technique he developed on this new *bağlama* type, the so-called *Dinç sazı* made by the luthier Süleyman Aslan, consists mainly of two fingernail techniques: classic arpeggio and the use of the index finger as a plectrum being a mix of guitar, tambour, and *bağlama* techniques. An example of this technique can be heard and seen on the innovative compositions on his CD/DVD *Bağlama için Denemeler* (Exercises for *Bağlama*).[172]

Execution Melody

Both horizontal and vertical playing techniques (*pozisyon*) can be used to play the melody.[173] In the big cities, both techniques have been combined, a development that has led to the development of both the short-necked *bağlama*, the *dört telli bağlama*, and *Oğur sazı*. In contrast to the long-necked *bağlama*, on which the melody is generally played on the first course and the others accompanying or produce the drone, the melody is performed over all courses (vertical movements), especially around the top of the neck, on both the short-necked *bağlama* and *dört telli bağlama*. The way of playing on the short-necked *bağlama* is generally limited to a number of relatively simple melodic cadences, with the intensive use of the middle course suggesting virtuosity and technical complexity.

Horizontal Techniques

The horizontal or linear playing technique, characteristic of the countryside of Anatolia, originated on traditional instruments on which there were only one, sometimes two, playing

---

[170] Eroğlu, S.C. Die Stellung der kopuz in der türkischen Volksmusic, in Çiftçi, N. and M. Greve (eds) Die Bağlama in der Türkei und Europa. Erstes Bağlama-Symposium in Deutschland. Berlin, 14-15 September 2013: 165, 167-169, 171; Erkan Oğur. Dönmez Yol (CD); Engin Topuzkanamış. Personal communication.
[171] Engin Topuzkanamış. Personal communication.
[172] Kemal Dinç. Personal communication.
[173] Stokes, M. The Arabesk Debate. Music and Musicians in Modern Turkey: 71-76.

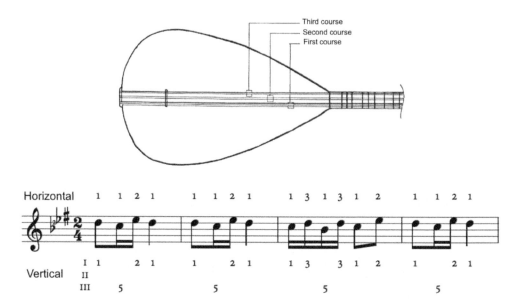

Figure 70. From bottom to top the first, second, and third course. The fingers are numbered as follows: 1 is the index finger, 2 the middle finger, 3 the ring finger, 4 the little finger, and 5 the thumb to shorten the third course. In the vertical playing technique, the number of movements along the neck can be minimized. Instead of playing the c on the first course, the c is played with the thumb on the third course. This principle can be applied to multiple positions on the neck.
© Author.

strings next to a bourdon string. The left hand moves up and down along the playing or melody string or course. The horizontal technique and the way in which the instrument is tuned enables bourdon playing and ornamenting the melody with *çarpmas*. Faster passages are mainly played around the top of the neck as the distance between the frets decreases from bottom to top.

Vertical Techniques

The vertical technique is mainly used in the big cities, where the possibility of systematically distributing the melody over all three courses is perceived as logical. The number of movements around the neck can thus be minimized. Instead of, for example, taking the c on the first course, this tone can also be obtained with the thumb on the third course. This principle can be applied to multiple positions of the neck. Some musicians of the current generation, such as Okan Murat Öztürk (1967) and Erkan Oğur (1954), use the vertical technique for playing harmonies on respectively the *dört telli bağlama* and the *Oğur sazı,*.

See YouTube for examples of playing techniques.

Glossary of Musical Instruments and Terms

Ağıt. Lamentation, *uzun hava.*

Altı telli saz. Name for a six-stringed Turkish long-necked lute.

Arabesk. Form of entertainment music that originated in the migrant neighbourhoods of the big cities, in particular Istanbul. The *arabesk* narrates the experiences of the migrants from Anatolia in the big cities.

Aras bağlama. Double-necked *bağlama.*

Atışma, tartışma, karşılama. Musical duels between *âşık.*

Aulos. A pair of slender pipes played together. By far the most important of the Greek wind Instruments of Antiquity.

Ayak. Tone system from Turkish folk music.

Âyîn-i djem. Ceremony of union of the Alevî and Bektaşi.

Baghlamádhes. Small Greek long-necked lutes.

Bağlama. Key instrument of the Turkish *bağlama* family.

Bağlama family. Cura, bağlama, tanbura, divan sazı, meydan sazı.

Balta sazı. Turkish long-necked lute with conic-shaped bowl.

Barbût. Ottoman short-necked lute.

Bas bağlama. Four-stringed bas version of the Turkish *bağlama.*

Bouzoúki. Greek three or four-course long-necked lute.

Bozlak. Song and poetic form (*uzun hava*).

Bozuk. Turkish long-necked lute.

Bulgarı. Turkish long-necked lute.

Çarpma. Hammering of the string or course by the second or third finger.

Cent. Measure to indicate the size of an octave or interval: an octave consists of 1200 cents, 100 cents for each semitone, according to the equal temperament.

Çeşte. Turkish long-necked lute.

Comma. The Turkish music theory uses the comma instead of the cent as a unit of measurement for the size of the intervals.

Çifte. Type of clarinet.

Çöğür. Large five-stringed Turkish long-necked lute.

Colascione. Italian long-necked lute (*tanbûr*).

Cümbüş. Sort of Turkish banjo.

Cura. Small Turkish long-necked lute.

Daire. Frame drum with small cymbals.

Dambura, dombrâ, dumbrâk. Uzbek and Tajik fretless *tanbûrs.*

Darbuka. Small Turkish drum.

Davul. Big drum.

Def. Tambourine.

Destan. Epic, balade.

Deyiş. Philosophical, religious, song, poetry (*uzun hava*)

Diatonic tone system. Seven-tone tone system consisting of five full and two half-tone distances.

Diliruba. Bowed string instrument from India.

Dinç sazı. Bağlama developed by Kemal Dinç in cooperation with the luthier Süleyman Aslan.

Divane. Turkish long-necked lute with a 'ûd-shaped bowl built in various sizes.

Divan sazı. Large Turkish long-necked lute.

Dört telli bağlama. Name for a four-course Turkish long-necked lute.

Dotâr, dutâr, dutôr. Names for various long-necked lutes in Iran and Central Asia.

Dömbra. Two-stringed fretless Kazakh *tanbûr.*

Dümbelek. Small drum.

Elektrobağlama. Amplified version of the *bağlama.*

Guitar-saz. Hybrid of a *saz* (neck) and guitar (body) built by the luthier Süleyman Aslan for Ahmet Aslan.

Iki telli saz. Name for a two-stringed long-necked lute in Anatolia.

Ilahi. Religious hymns (*uzun hava*)

Irızva. Small Turkish long-necked lute with conic-shaped bowl.

Kanun, kanûn, qânûn. Trapezium-shaped cither.

Karadüzen. Turkish long-necked lute. Also name of a *saz* tuning.

Karar sesi. End tone, the tone which one of the courses (string groups) must produce and to which the other courses are tuned.

Kaşık. Spoons.

Kaval. Shepperd's flute.

Kayabaşı. Song and poetic form (*uzun hava*).

Kemane. Fiddle.

Kemenche (Arabic), *kemânçe* (Ottoman), *kamânça* (Persian). Spike fiddle with a small, often spherical, resonating chamber.

Kırık hava. Broken melody, less common than the *uzun hava.*

Kısa saplı bağlama. Turkish short-necked long-necked lute.

Kopuz, qobyz, gobuz. Short-necked Turkish folk lute. In modern Central Asia in the form of *qobyz* for a fiddle used by the shamans and epic bards in Kazakhstan and Karakalpakia.

Kopuz-i ozan. Kopuz of the *ozan* (poet-musicians).

Kopuz-i rûmî. The Turkish of Byzantine *kopuz.*

Kopuzıla çeşte. Six-stringed *kopuz.*

Koşma. Song and poetic form (*uzun hava*).

Makam. Tone system of Ottoman classical music.

Mani. Improvised texts in the form of a single stanza.

Maya. Song and poetic form (*uzun hava*).

Melisma. Melodies sung in small note values or sequences of tones on a single syllable.

Mersiye. Religious mourning song; poetry (*uzun hava*).

Methiye. Song and poetic form; poetry (*uzun hava*).

Metrum. The regularity in the musical time movement. The extent to which the actual musical movement exhibits a metric character can vary greatly. Sometimes the contours of the musical movement of time and the metric cadence coincide entirely - one speaks of a bound rhythm (i.e. *kırık hava*) - then again there is hardly any regularity in the rhythmic progress - the free rhythm (i.e. *uzun hava*).

Mey. Shepperd's pipe, shawn

Meydan sazı. Largest Turkish long-necked lute.

Microtone. Interval less than a quarter tone; microtones are important in the *uzun hava.*

Mıskal. Ottoman panpipes. Abandoned during the 1st half of the 18th century.

Müzik kalıbı or *şiir kalıbı.* Musical or poetic form (*ayak*).

Nakkare, naqqâra. Kettle drums.

Nây, ney. End-blown flute in the Arab world, Iran, and Turkey.

Nefes. Hymn, mystical form of poetry and song created in the Bektaşî *tekes*, poetry.

Oğur sazı. Turkish long-necked lute built in various designs after an idea of Erkan Oğur.

Octave. The eighth tone rising or falling from the root. Almost all tone systems that occur in the world know the phenomenon of octave. However, they differ from one another in the way they select and locate pitches within the octave.

On telli saz. Name for a ten-stringed Turkish long-necked lute.

Ottoman *kopuz.* Short-necked lute of the Ottoman *makam* tradition.

Ottoman *tanbûr.* Ottoman *tanbûr* of the Ottoman *makam* tradition.

Pandoura (pandouros, phandouros, pandouris, pandourion). Greek long-necked lute.

Perdesiz tanbura. Fretless Turkish *saz.*

Qobuz, qobyz, gyl-gobyz. Central Asian fiddle.

Quarter tone. Interval the size of half a half-pitch.

Rabâb. Plucked or bowed long-necked lute with a stretched skin top.

Rûh-efzâ or *gıdâ-yi rûh* ('food of soul or spirit'). Tanbûr invented by the Ottoman prince (Korkut.

Šargija, šargkija. Long-necked lute played in the folk music of various south-eastern countries.

Şarkı. Turkish long-necked lute.

Saz, sâz. Turkish and Azerbaijani long-necked lute, generic name for musical instruments.

Sáze. Albanian long-necked lute.

Saz şairleri. Poets with a *saz.*

Şelpe. Finger technique including two forms of 'fret taping': the *parmak vurma tekniği* (hammering) and the *tel çekme tekniği* (pulling).

Sema. Religious dance.

Semai. Song and poetic form in Ottoman classical music and *âşık* poetry.

Semi akustik bağlama. Amplified Turkish *bağlama* with flat openwork body.

Şeşde. Turkish long-necked lute.

Şeştâr. Persian six-stringed long-necked lute.

Setâr. Four-stringed Iranian long-necked lute.

Sipsi. Small shepherd's flute.

Spike lute. Long-necked lute with a tortoise shell or wooden resonator and a rod-shaped neck.

Sünder. Turkish long-necked lute.

Syllabic melody. Melody that has one tone for each syllable.

Tambura, tanbura. Turkish long-necked lute.

Tambura. Generic name in south-eastern Europe for long-necked lutes. The smaller-sized forms are indicated by the diminutive *tamburica* (*tamburče* in Macedonia). In scientific literature a name to distinguish the Eastern European varieties of the Turkish long-necked lute (*saz*).

Tambourádhes. Generic name for long-necked lutes in Greece.

Tanbour baghlama. Small four-stringed long-necked lute (Egypt).

Tanbour boulghâry. Small four-stringed long-necked lute (Egypt).

Tanbour bouzork. Large six-stringed long-necked lute (Egypt).

Tanbour chargy. Large four-stringed long-necked lute (Egypt).

Tanbûr. General name for long-necked lutes of art, mystical and folk musical traditions.

Tanbûr al-baghdâdî (or *mîzânî*). Two-stringed Abbâsid long-necked lute.

Tanbûr al-khurasânî. Two-stringed Umayyad/Abbâsid long-necked lute.

Tanbûr-i şirvâniyân. Two-stringed Tîmûrid long-necked lute.

Tanbûre-i tûrkî. Two-stringed Turkish long-necked lute.

Teltanbûrası. Turkish long-necked lute.

Tread cime. The distance in pitch between a tone and the subsequent thirteenth tone.

Tunbûr. Two-stringed Sâsânian *tunbûr*, mutated by the Arabs to *tanbûr*.

Türkü. Song and poetry form, folksong (*uzun hava*).

Üç telli. Name for a three-stringed Turkish long-necked lute.

Üç telli bağlama. Name for a small three-stringed *bağlama.*

'Ûd. Arabic short-necked lute found in various versions throughout the Islamic world.

Uzun hava. Long melody, the *uzun hava* is rhythmically free and therefore offers room for improvisation and ornamentation.

Uzun saplı bağlama. Long-necked Turkish *bağlama.*

Varsağı. Songs that take their name from the Varsak, a tribe from the Taurus Mountains, *uzun hava.*

Yaren sazı. Triple-necked Turkish long-necked lute.

Yedi telli saz. Name for a seven-stringed Turkish long-necked lute.

Yeltme. Turkish long-necked lute.

Yonkar. Turkish long-necked lute.

Zil. Metal castanets.

Zurna. A double-reed, conical-bore oboe.

Zeybek. Accompanying music with men's dance.

Discography

From the sixties of the last century, audio cassettes became the most important medium for distributing music. The production costs were low and they could be played on simple and inexpensive cassette recorders. The cassettes are distributed via a network consisting of small music shops, but also in shopping arcades, at bus stations, and quays for ferries, etc. Towards the end of the last century we also see the number of CD recordings increasing increasingly replacing the cassettes.

In the meantime, there are increasingly less CD releases, for which there are many reasons. Lesser interest in 'world music' is surely one of them. The main reason, however, is that the main way of buying and listening to music is via commercial downloads and streaming services. The younger generations don't buy CDs anymore. Then there is also the fact that practical everything is available for free as piracy downloads or on YouTube. For example, when a new CD is published, a couple of days later you find it somewhere on an internet site to be downloaded for free. Everywhere the music industry is down seizing, not only in the West, but also in Turkey and even in Iran and especially in India, where the production of CDs with traditional music is really dramatic. In 2016, however, profits from music streaming, first by *Spotify* and later also by *Apple* and *Amazon*, gave some labels their largest rise in revenues in more than a decade. Unfortunately, not the entire music industry has benefited from streaming.[174]

Akarsu, Muhlis. *Ölümsüz Ozanlar Serisi 1*. Ömüzik San CD -.
Akarsu, Muhlis. *Ölümsüz Ozanlar Serisi 2*. Ömüzik San CD -.
Akarsu, Muhlis. *Âşık Olan Durmaz Ağlar*. Kalan CD-125.
Albayrak Hüseyin, Albayrak Ali Riza. *Şah Hatayi Deyişleri*. Kalan CD 326.
Altunsaray, Ismail. *Incidir*. Kalan CD 553.
Arif Sağ Trio. *Concerto for Bağlama*. ASM Müzik Üretim CD 021.
Âşık Ali Izzet Özkan. *Mecnunum Leylamı Gördum*. Kalan CD 194.
Âşık Veysel. Kalan CD 235-236.
Âşık Veysel. *Bana da Banaz'da Pir Sultan Derler*. Kalan CD 738.
Aslan, Ahmet. *Na-Mükemmel. Imperfect*. Kalan CD 695
Aslan, Ahmet and Kemal Dinç. *Duo*. Kalan CD 736.
Asya Içlerinden Balkanlara. Saz. Kalan CD 077.
Baraná & Co. *Live at the Music Meeting*. LopLop Records, LLr-01.
Başaran, Refik. *Şen Olasın Ürgüp*. Kalan CD 217.
Bayram Aracı. *Alli Yazma*. Kalan CD 206
Bektâşî Nefesleri 1. *The Bektashi Breathes 1*. Cemre CD 101.
Bektâşî Nefesleri 2. *The Bektashi Breathes 2*. Cemre CD 102.
Bektâşî Nefesleri 3. *The Bektashi Breathes 3*. Cemre CD 137.
Bengi Bağlama Üçlüsü. *Güneş Bahçesinden Ezgiler*. Kalan CD 119.
Bengi Bağlama Üçlüsü. *Sel gider...kum kalır....* Kalan CD 208

---

[174] Ellis-Petersen, H. Music streaming hailed as industry's saviour as labels enjoy profit surge. Guardian, 29 December 2016. Elbin, A. Raga, Maqam, Dastgah. Traditional Music from India and the Islamic World on CD. Düsseldorf. Personal communication.

Çekiç, Ali. *Kızılırmak*. Kalan CD 152.

Çiçek, Ali Ekber. *Turkey. Bektashi Music. Ashik Songs.* Auvidis/Unesco CD D 8069.

Çimen, Nesimî. *Ayrılık Hasreti*. Kalan CD 283-284.

Çırakman, Hüseyin. *Bugün Hoşgeldiniz Erenler*. Kalan CD 219.

Dem Trio. *The Fountain – Turkish Musical Traditions.* Felmay FY 8133.

Dinç, Kemal and Chamber Music Ensemble Drama. *Lir ve Ateş*. Kalan CD 375.

Dinç, Kemal. *Bağlama Için Denemler* (CD&DVD). Kalan CD 573.

Eroğlu, Musa, Muhlis Akarsu, Yavuz Top. *Muhhabbet-6*. Kalan CD 032.

Eroğlu, Musa, Muhlis Akarsu, Yavuz Top. *Muhhabbet-7*. Kalan CD 033.

Eroğlu, Musa, Arif Sağ. *Turquie. Musique Instrumentale d'Anatolie.* Buda Records – Musique du Monde CD 92620-2.

Ertaş, Muharrem. *Kalktı Göç Eyledi*. Kalan CD 112.

Ertaş, Muharrem. *Başımda Altın Tacım*. Kalan CD 183.

Ertaş, Neşet. *Zülüf Dökülmüş Yüze*. Kalan CD 137.

Ertaş, Neşet. *Gönül Dağı*. Kalan CD 138.

Ertaş, Neşet. *Mühür Gözlüm*. Kalan CD 139.

Ertaş, Neşet. *Zahidem*. Kalan CD 140.

Ertaş, Neşet. *Garibin Dünyada Yüzü Gülemez*. Kalan CD 166.

Ertaş, Neşet. *Niye Çattın Kaşlarını*. Kalan CD 167.

Ertaş, Neşet. *Çiçek Dağı*. Kalan CD 168.

Ertaş, Neşet. *Ayaşyolları*. Kalan CD 169.

Ertaş, Neşet. *Sevsem Öldürürler*. Kalan CD 191.

Ertaş, Neşet. *Ağla Sazım*. Kalan CD 192.

Ertaş, Neşet. *Hatabenim*. Kalan CD 193.

Ertaş, Neşet. *Dostlara Selam*. Kalan CD 214.

Ertaş, Neşet. *Sabreyle Gönül*. Kalan CD 215.

Ertaş, Neşet. *Neşet Ertaş in Concert*. Kalan DVD 03.

Ertaş, Neşet. *Garip. Neşet Ertaş Belgeseli*. Kalan DVD 05.

Erzincan, Erdal. *Şelpe*. Temkes CD 006.

Erzincan, Mercan. *Gökkusağı*. Temkeş Müzik CD -.

Evren Hacıoğlu, Mehmet. *Dâmen*. ASC CD -.

Gönlüm, Özay. *Özay Gönlüm Arşiv Kayıtları*. Kalan CD 335-336.

Gülâ, Coşkun. *Bağlamada Tezene Tavırları*. Kalan CD 170.

Gültekin, Hasret. *Secmeler 1*. Kalan CD 012.

Güngör, Fethiyeli Ramazan. *Ve Üç Telli Bağlamasi*. Kalan CD 079.

Hisarlı Ahmet. *Kütahya'nın Pınarları*. Kalan CD 056

Kadın Âşıklar. Kalan CD 504.

Kalhor, Kalhor, Erdal Erzincan. *The Wind*. ECM Records CD 1981.

Kalhor, Kalhor, Erdal Erzincan. *Kula Kulluk Yakışır Mı*. ECM Records CD 2181.

Karademir, Coşkun and Emirhan Kartal. *Sırdask*. Kalan CD-595.

Le Baglama des Yayla. Ocora C 560213.

Oğur, Erkan. *Bir Ömürlük Misafir*. Kalan CD 184.

Oğur, Erkan. *Dönmez Yol*. Kalan CD 565

Oğur, Erkan and Ismail Hakkı Demiroğlu. *Gülün Kokusu Vardi*. Kalık Müzik Yapım CD 086.

Oğur, Erkan and Ismail Hakkı Demiroğlu. *Anadolu Beşik*. Kalan CD 178.

Oğur, Erkan and Okan Murat Öztürk. *Hiç*. Kalan CD 135.

Özkan, Cengiz and Muharrem Temiz. *Yare Dokunma*. Kalan CD 239.

Özkan, Cengiz. *Saklarım Gözümde Güzelliğini*. Kalan CD 269.

Özkan, Talip. *Mysteries of Turkey*. Music of the World CD T 115.

Özkan, Talip. *Turquie. L'art Vivant de Talip Özkan*. Ocora C 580047.

Özkan, Talip. *Turquie. L'art du Tanbûr*. Ocora C 560042.

Öztürk, Okan Murat. *Turkish Authentic Saz*. Mega Müzik CD 034.

Öztürk, Okan Murat. *Eski Havalar*. Mega Müzik CD 047.

Öztürk, Okan Murat. *Aşk Adamı Söyletir*. Rec CD 20049.

Öztürk, Okan Murat. *Bergüzar*. DMC CD 20080.

Parlak, Erol. *Erol Parlak Bağlama Beşlisi*. Arda Müzik CD -.

Rumeli Bektaşîleri. Kalan CD 190.

Sağ, Arif. *Gurbeti Ben mi Yarattım*. Kalan CD 105.

Şerif, Mahsunî. *İste Gidiyorum Çeşme Siyahım*. Emre CD H.E.091.

Şerif, Mahsunî, Musa Eroğlu, Ashik Bahattin Kader, Ashik Nuri Kiliç and Ashik Ali. *Ashiklar, those who are in Love*. Golden Horn GHP 010-2.

Song Creators in Eastern Turkey. Smithsonian Folkways Recordings SF40432.

Sularî, Davut. *Bugün Bayram Günü Derler*. Kalan 175.

Taşan, Hacı. *Allı Turnam*. Kalan CD 126.

Taşan, Hacı. *Yüce Dağ Başında*. Kalan CD 145.

Taşan, Hacı. *Çok Zaman Sabrettim*. Kalan CD 146.

Top, Yavuz. *Suçumuz Nedir*. Ses Plak CD -.

Top, Yavuz. *Hazan Değdi*. BAY CD 052.

Tüfekçi, Nida. *Sürmeli*. Kalan CD 106.

Tschinar, Ashik Feyzullah. *Turquie. Chants Sacrés d'Anatolie*. Ocora C 580057.

Turkish Folk Songs and Instrumental Music. World Music Library. King Records KICC 5102.

Turquie - Aşik. *Chants d'Amour et de Sagesse d'Anatolie*. Inédit W 260025.

Turquie. *Asie mineure. Anatolie - Musique profane*. Al Sur ALCD 130.

Turquie. *Cérémonie des Derviches Kadiri*. VDE-GALLO CD 587.

Turquie. *Musique des Troubadours. Ozan Fırat*. Ethnic B 6771

Turquie. *Cérémonie du Djem Alevi*. Ocora C 560125.

Turquie. *Cérémonie de Djem Bektashi. La tradition d'Abdal Musa*. Turkey. Ocora C 560248.

Turquie. *La Cérémonie des Derviches de Konya*. VDE-GALLO CD 1324.

Turquie. *Musiques des Yayla*. Ocora C 560050.

Turquie. *Musiques Villageoises d'Anatolie*. VDE-GALLO CD 797.

Turquie. *Asie Mineure. Anatolie – Musique Profane. Adnan Ataman, Arif Sağ, Binali Selman*. Al Sur. ALCD 130.

Uzelli Elektro Saz (1976-1984). Uzelli Records, CD 1324-2.

Bibliography

Abraham, G. 1979. *The Concise Oxford History of Music*. Oxford: Oxford University Press.

Açin, C. 1994. *Enstruman Bilimi (Organoloji)*. Istanbul: Yenidoğan Basımevi.

Açin, C. 2000. *Bağlama. Yapım sanatı ve sanatçıları*. Istanbul: Emek Basımevi.

Açin, C. 2002. *Tanbûr. Yapım sanatı ve sanatçıları*. Istanbul: Bilgi Basımevi.

Akdağ, A.K. 2012. *Bağlamada Düzenler ve Tezene Tavırları*. Istanbul: Pan Yayıncılık.

Akdoğu, O. 1999. *Türk müziğinde perdeler*. Ankara: Müzik Ansiklopedisi Yayınları.

Akyıldız, A. 2017. *Haremin Padişahı. Valide Sultan. Harem'de Hayat ve Teşkilat*. Istanbul: Timaş Yayınları.

Aksoy, B. 2003. *Avrupalı gezginlerin gözüyle Osmanlılarda musikî*. Istanbul: Pan Yayıncılık.

Al-Farâbî, Abû Nasr. 1930, 1935. *Grand traité de la musique. Kitâbu l-Mûsîqî al-Kabir: La musique arabe*, Vols. 1 and 2. Baron Rodolphe Erlanger (Trans.). Paris: Libraire orientaliste Paul Geuthner.

Al-Farâbî, Abû Nasr. 1998. *Kitâb al-Mûsîqî al-Kabîr*. E. Neubauer (ed.). Frankfurt: Institut für Geschichte der Arabisch-Islamischen Wissenschaften (Goethe Universität).

Al-Fârûqî, L.I. 1981. *An Annotated Glossary of Arabic Musical Terms*. Westport (Conecticut): Greenwood Press.

Al-Fârûqî, L.I. 1985. Music, Musicians and Muslim Law. *Asian Music* 17: 3-37.

Ali Ufkî Bey / Albertus Bobovius. *Saray-ı Enderun. Topkapı Sarayı'nda Yaşam*. Noyan, T. (transl.) 2013. Istanbul: Kitap Yayınevi.

Al-Marâghî, Abd al-Qadir Ibnu Ghaibî 1977. *Maqâsid al-Alhân*. Taqi Binish (ed.). Teheran: Zendegi.

Al-Marâghî, Abd al-Qadir Ibnu Ghaibî 1987. *Jâmi' al-Alhân*. Taqi Binish (ed.). Teheran: Mash'al.

Alpay, G. 1972. XV. Yüzyil Ilk Yarısında Yazılmış Münazara: Sazlar Münazarası. *Araştırma Ankara* Üniversitesi *Dil ve Tarih-Coğrafya Fakültesi Felsefe Bölümü Dergisi* X: 99-132.

Altan, S. 2013. *Konzert für Bağlama und Orchester*. Berlin. Ries und Erler.

Altan, S. 2013. *Mr. Sax in Anatolia, Konzert für Saxophon Solo Orchester, Bağlama und Mey*. Berlin: Ries und Erler.

And, M. 2014. *Ottoman Figurative Arts 1: Miniature*. Istanbul: Yapı Kredi Yayınları.

And, M. 2018 (Geğirmenci, T. and M. Sabri Koz, eds). *Ottoman Figurative Arts 2: Bazaar Painters*. Istanbul: Yapı Kredi Yayınları.

And, M. 2020. *Karagöz. Turkish Shadow Theatre*. Istanbul: Yapı Kredi Yayınları.

Anderson, R., S. El-Shawan Castelo-Branco and V. Danielson 2001. Egypt, in S. Sadie (ed.) *New Grove Dictionary of Music and Musicians* 8: 1-17. London: MacMillan Press Limited.

Anoyanakis, F. 1965. Ein byzantinisches Instrument. *Acta musicoligica* XXXVII: 158-165.

Anoyanakis, F. 1991. *Greek popular musical instruments*. Greece: Melissa Publishing House.

Apan, V. 2000. Romania, in T. Rice, J. Porter and C. Goertzen (eds) *The Garland Encyclopedia of World Music. Europe* Volume 8. London and New York: Routledge.

Appadurai, A. 1996. *Modernity at Large: Cultural Dimensions of Globalization*. Mineapolis: University of Minnesota Press.

Arık, R. 2000. *Kubad Abad. Selçuklu Sarayı ve Çinileri*. Istanbul: Türkiye İş Bankası Kültür Yayınları.

Aruz, J. (ed.) 2003. *Art of the First Cities. The Third Millennium BC from the Mediterranean to the Indus*. New York: The Metropolitan Museum of Art. New Haven and London: Yale University Press.

Aruz, J., K. Benzell and J.M. Evans (eds) 2008. *Beyond Babylon. Art, Trade, and Diplomacy in the Second Millennium BC.* New York: The Metropolitan Museum of Art. New Haven and London: Yale University Press.

Asadi, H. 2002. Musical Instruments in Timûrid Paintings: An Organological Approach. *The Journal of Humanities of the Islamic Republic of Iran* 9 (3): 1-25.

Ataman, S.Y. 1938. *Anadolu halk sazları yerli musikiciler ve halk musiki karakterleri.* Istanbul: Burhaneddin Matbaası.

Ataman, A. 2009. *Bu Toprağın Sesi. Halk Musikimiz.* Istanbul: Türk Edebiyatı Vakfı Yayınları.

Ataman, S.Y. 1938. *Anadolu halk sazları yerli musikiciler ve halk musiquei karakterleri.* Istanbul.

Atanasov, V. 1983. *Die bulgarischen Volksmusikinstrumente: eine Systematik in Wort, Bild und Ton.* München: Musikverlag Emil Katzbichler.

Atasoy, N. 1997. *Surname-i Hümayun. An Imperial Celebration.* Istanbul: Koçbank.

Atasoy, N. 2011. *Harem.* Ankara: Bilkent Kültür Girişimi Publications.

Atıl, E. 1986. *Süleymanname. The Illustrated History of Süleyman the Magnificient.* New York: Harry N. Abrams.

Atıl, E. 1987. *The Age of Sultan Süleyman the Magnificent.* New York: Harry N. Abrams.

Atıl, E. 1999. *Levni and the Surname. The Story of an Eighteenth-Century Ottoman Festival.* Istanbul: Koçbank.

Aydemir, M. 2015. *Turkish Maqam Guide (2 CDs).* Istanbul: Pan Yayıncılık.

Bachmann, W. and B. Dinçol 2001. Anatolia, in S. Sadie (ed.) *New Grove Dictionary of Music and Musicians* 1: 589-603. London: MacMillan Press.

Bağcı, S., F. Çağman, G. Renda and Z. Tanıdı 2000. *Ottoman Painting.* Turkey: Republic of Turkey Ministry of Culture and Tourism Publications.

Baines, A. 1950. Tinctoris : De inventione et usu musicae. *Journal of the Galpin Society* 3: 19-26. London.

Baines, A. 1992. *The Oxford Companion to Musical Instruments.* Oxford: Oxford University Press.

Baldick, J. 2012. *Mystical Islam. An Introduction to Sufism.* London: I.B. Tauris.

Barth, D. 2008. *Etnnie, Bildung oder Bedeutung? Zum Kulturbegriff in der interkulturell orientierten Musikpädagogik.* Augsburg: Wißner Verlag.

Başgöz, I. 1952. Turkish Folk Stories about the Lives of Minstrels. *The Journal of American Folklore* 65 (258): 331-339.

Başgöz, I. 1998. More about politics and folklore in Turkey. *The Journal of American Folklore* 111: 413-415.

Bartók, B. 1976. *Turkish Folk Music from Asia Minor.* B. Suchoff (ed.). Princeton: Princeton University Press.

Bates, E. 2011. *Music in Turkey: Experiencing Music, Expressing Culture (Global Music Series).* Oxford: Oxford University Press.

Bates, E. 2012. The Social Life of Musical Instruments. *Ethnomusicology* 56 (3): 365-395.

Baumann, M.P. 2006. *Musik im interkulturellen Kontext.* Nordhausen: Traugott Bautz.

Bayrak, M. 2005. *Ermeni Âşıkları [Aşuğlar].* Alevi-Bektaşi Edebiyatında. Ankara: Öz-Ge Yayınları.

Beckwith, C.I. 2009. *Empires of the Silk Road: A History of Central Asia from the Bronze Age to the Present.* Princeton: Princeton University Press.

Behar, C. 2006. The Ottoman musical tradition, in S. Faroqhi (ed.) *The Cambridge History of Turkey. Volume 3. The Later Ottoman Empire, 1603-407:* 393-407. Cambridge: Cambridge University Press.

Behar, C. 2008. *Musıkiden Müziğe. Osmanlı/Türk Müziği: Gelenek ve Modernlik.* Istanbul: Yapı Kredi Yayınları.

Beljaev, V. 1933. *Muzykal'nye Instrumenty Uzbekistana*. Moscow.

Bent, J.Th. (ed.) 1893. *Early Voyages and Travels in the Levant. II Extracts from the Diaries of Dr John Covel, 1670-1679*: 99-289. London: Hakluyt Society.

Bentley, J.H. 1996. Cross-Cultural Interaction and Periodization in World History. *The American Historical Review* 101 (3): 749-770.

Beyer, N. 1998. Tambūrā, in L. Finscher (ed.) *Die Musik in Geschichte und Gegenwart. Allgemeine Enzyklopädie der Musik* 23: 217-221. Kassel, Basel, Paris, London, New York, Prag: Bärenreiter/ Stuttgart, Weimar: Melzler.

Bezić, J., M. Gavazzi, M. Jakelić and P. Mihanović 1975. *Tradicijska Narodna Glazbala Jugoslavije* (Traditional Folk Musical Instruments of Jugoslavia). Zagreb.

Blainville, C-H. de 1776. *Histoire générale, critique et philologique de la musique*. Paris: Pisot.

Blum, L. 2001. Geste instrumental et transmission musicale. *Cahiers d'ethnomusicologie* 14: 237-248.

Blažeković, Z. Illustrations of Musical Instruments in Jean-Benjamine de Laborde's *Essai sur la musique ancienne et moderne*, in Musique, Images, Instruments. Revue française d'organologie et d'iconographie musicale 15. Portraits, ballets, traités: 149.

Blum, S. 1972. The concept of asheq in northern Khorâsân. *Journal of the Society for Asian Music* 4: 27-48.

Blum, S., D. Christensen and A. Shiloah 2001a. Kurdish Music, in S. Sadie (ed.) *New Grove Dictionary of Music and Musicians* 14: 36-41. London: MacMillan Press Limited.

Blum, S. 2001b. Central Asia, in S. Sadie (ed.) *New Grove Dictionary of Music and Musicians* 5: 363-372. London: MacMillan Press Limited.

Bobowski, W. (Ali Ufkî Bey) 1976. *Mecmû'a-i sâz ü söz*. Ş. Elçin (ed.). Istanbul: Kültür Bakanlığı.

Bonanni, F. 1964. *Antique Musical Instruments and their Players*, reprint of *Gabinetto Armonico*, Roma 1723. New York: Dover Publications.

Bonanni, F. 1975. *Descrizione degli'ístromenti armonico d'ogni genere del Padre Bonnani*. Secunda edizione riveduta, coretta, ed accresciuta dall'abate Giacinto Cerutti ornate con CXL rami incise d'Arnoldo Wanwesterout. Roma: Venanzio Monaldini 1776. Nachdr. Kassel: Bârenreiter.

Bowersock, G.W., P. Brown, and Grabar, O. 1999. Late Antiquity, A Guide to the Postclassical World. Cambridge, Massachuzetts, and London: The Belknap Press of Harvard University Press.

Brandl, R. 1976. Über das Phänomen Bordun (Drone). *Studien zur Musik SO-Europas, Beiträge zur Ethnomusicologie* 4: 90-121.

Brandl, R.M. 2000. Bordun, in L. Finscher (ed.) *Die Musik in Geschichte und Gegenwart. Allgemeine Enzyklopädie der Musik* 2: 69-75. Kassel, Basel, Paris, London, New York, Prag: Bärenreiter/ Stuttgart, Weimar: Melzler.

Braune, G. 1989. Musik in Orient und Okzident. G. Sievernich and H. Budde (eds). *Europa in Orient und Okzident*. Berliner Festspiele: 210-230. Gütersloh: Bertelsmann Lexicon Verlag.

Bryant, R. 2005. The soul danced into the body: nation and improvisation in Istanbul. *American Ethnologist* 32 (2): 222-238.

Buchner, A. 1981. *Handbuch der Musikinstrumente*. Hanau: Dausien.

Bull, D. 2002. Jean-Etienne Liotard (1702-1789). Rijksmuseum Dossiers. Amsterdam, Rijksmuseum Amsterdam.

Çağatay, E. and D. Kuban 2007. *The Turkic Speaking Peoples. 2,000 Years of Art and Culture from Inner Asia to the Balkans*. München: Prestel and Prins Claus Fund Library.

Çak, S.E. and Ş.Ş Beşiroğlu 2017. Kadın ve Müzik. Istanbul: Milenyum Yayınları.

Çalka, M.S. 2008. Nev'î Divânı'nda Mûsikî Terimleri. *Turkish Studies. International Periodical For the Languages Literature and History of Turkish or Turkic* 3/2: 179-193.

Campbell, R.G. 1970. *Zur Typologie der Schalenlanghalslaute*. Strasbourg, Baden-Baden: Verlag Heitz.

Canby, S.R., D. Beyazit, M. Rugladi and A.C.S. Peacock 2016. *Court and Cosmos: The Great Age of the Seljuks*. New Haven and London: Yale University Press.

Canfield, R.L. (ed.) 2002. *Turko-Persia in Historical Perspective*. Cambridge: Cambridge University Press.

Catalog of the Musical Instrument Collection of the Koizumi Fumio Memorial Archives Faculty of Music 1987. Tokyo: Tokyo Geijutsu Daigaku.

Çetin, K. 2009. Musikî ve Musikî Terimlerinin Ibrahim Râşid Divânı'ndaki Yansımaları. *Turkish Studies. International Periodical for the Languages Literature and History of Turkish or Turkic* 4: 2199-2225.

Chelebi, E. 1976. *Turkish Instruments of Music in the Seventeenth Century. As described in the Siyahat Nama of Ewliya Chelebi*. H.G. Farmer (transl. and ed.). Portland (Maine): Longwood Press.

Chouquet, G. 1875. *Le Musée du Conservatoire National de Musique. Catalogue raisonné des instruments de cette collection*. Paris: Firmin-Didot.

Çiftçi, N. and M. Greve (eds) 2017. *Die Bağlama in der Türkei und Europa. Erstes Bağlama Symposium in Deutschland. Berlin, 14-15. September 2013*. Berlin: Ries & Erler.

Çiftçi, N. 2017. Klassifizierung der in Anatolien gespieten Bağlama-Famile in terminologischer, typologischer und tonräumlicher Hinsicht, in Çiftçi, N. and M. Greve (eds) *Die Bağlama in der Türkei und Europa. Erstes Bağlama-Symposium in Deutschland. Berlin, 14-15 September 2013*: 17-36.

Çiftçi, N. Bezeichnungen und Definitionen traditioneller Langhalslauten im Wörterbuch *Türkçe Sözlük* der Türkischen Sprachgesellschaft (TDK) seit 1945 du ihre Rezeption in der deutschen Sprache- und Musikforschung, in Çiftçi, N. and M. Greve (eds) *Die Bağlama in der Türkei und Europa. Erstes Bağlama-Symposium in Deutschland. Berlin, 14-15 September 2013*: 103-142.

Çinar, S. 2008. *Yirminci Yüzyılın Ikinic Yasında Türkiye'de* Âşıklar *Female* Âşıks in Turkey in the Second *Halve of the Twentieth Century)*. Ankara: Yayınlanmamış Dotora Tezi. ITÜ Sosyal Bilimler Enstitüsü.

Clark, M. 2005. *Sound of the Silk Road: Musical Instruments of Asia*. Boston: Museum of Fine Arts.

Cler, J. 2000. *Musique du Turquie*. CD7111. Arles, Paris: Actes Sud/Cité de la Musique.

Cler, J. 2011. *Yayla. Musique et Musiciens de Villages en Turquie Méridionale*. Paris: Geuthner.

Colon, D. and A.D. Kilmer 1980. The Lute in Ancient Mesopotamia. *Music and Civilisation*. The British Museum Yearbook 4: 13-23.

Conrad, J. 1998. The Political Face of Folklore. A Call for a Debate. *The Journal of American Folklore* 11: 409-413.

Conway Morris, R. 2001. Bağlama, in S. Sadie (ed.) *New Grove Dictionary of Music and Musicians* 2: 469. London: MacMillan Press Limited.

Cosma, O., A. Şirli, S. Radulescu and A. Guirschescu 2001. Romania, in S. Sadie (ed.) *New Grove Dictionary of Music and Musicians* 21: 581-594. London: MacMillan Press Limited.

Cowan, J.K. 2000. Greece, in T. Rice, J. Porter and C. Goertzen (eds) *The Garland Encyclopedia of World Music. Europe* Volume 8. London and New York: Routledge.

Dale, S.F. 2010. *The Muslim Empires of the Ottomans, Safavids, and Mughals*. Cambridge: Cambridge University Press.

Dankoff, R. and S. Kim 2010. *An Ottoman Traveller. Selections from the Book of Travels of Evliya Çelebi*. London: Eland Publishing Limited.

Darvishi, M-R. 2001. *Encyclopaedia of the Musical Instruments of Iran. Vol I. Chordophones in Regional Music* [Persian]. Teheran: Mahoor Institute of Culture and Art.

Denny, W.B. 1985. Music and Musicians in Islamic Art. *Asian Music. Journal of the Society for Asian Music* 17: 37-68.

Devale, S.C. 1988. Musical Instruments and Ritual: A Systematic Approach. *Journal of the American Musical Instrument Society* 5: 89-123.

Devič, D., B. Pejovic and J. Sugarman 2001. Yugoslavia, in S. Sadie (ed.) *New Grove Dictionary of Music and Musicians* 27: 685-696. London: MacMillan Press Limited.

Dietrich W. and B. Fosshag 1992. *Außereuropäische Lauten. Werkzeug & Kunstwerk. Sammlung Bengt Fosshag.* Frankfurt.

Djani-Zade, T. 2004. Die organologische und ikonographische Gestalt der türkischen Lauten. Über das historische Zupfinstrument qâpâz-i ôz. *Studia Instrumentorum Musicae Popularis XV.* International Council for Traditional Music Study Group on Folk Musical Instruments. Proceedings from the 15th International Meeting in Falun, Sweden August 14-18: 63-87. D. Lundberg and G. Ternhag (eds). Stockholm: Svenskt Visarkiv.

Doğan-Alparslan, M. and M. Alparslan 2013. *Hititler. Hittites. Bir Anadolu Imparatorluğu. An Anatolian Empire.* Istanbul: Yapı Kredi Yayınları.

Dolidze, L., C. Hannick, D. Dolidze, G. Chkikvadze and J. Jordania 2001. Georgia, in S. Sadie (ed.) *New Grove Dictionary of Music and Musicians* 9: 665-680. London: MacMillan Press.

Doubleday, V. 1992. Sounds of Power: An Overview of Musical Instruments and Gender. *Ethnomusicology Forum* 17 (1): 33-39.

Draffkorn Kilmer, A. 2001. Mesopotamia, in S. Sadie (ed.) *New Grove Dictionary of Music and Musicians* 16: 480-487. London: MacMillan Press Limited.

Duchesne-Guillemin, M. 1993. *Les instruments de musique dans l'art Sassanide. Iranica Antiqua.* Supplément VI, Gent.

Dugot, J. 2006. *Les luths (Occident). Catalogue des collections du Museé de la Musique.* Paris: Cité de la Musique.

Dumbrill, R.J. 2005. *The Archeomusicology of the Ancient Near East.* Bloomington (Indiana): Trafford Publishing.

During, J. 1989. *Musique et mystique dans les traditions de l'Iran.* Bibliotheque Iranienne 36. Paris – Téhéran: Institut Français de Recherche en Iran.

During, J. 2000a. Iran, in L. Finscher (ed.) *Die Musik in Geschichte und Gegenwart. Allgemeine Enzyklopädie der Musik* 13: 1164-1188. Kassel, Basel, Paris, London, New York, Prag: Bärenreiter/Stuttgart, Weimar: Melzler.

During, J., R. Sultanova and A. Djumaev 2000b. Zentralasien, in L. Finscher (ed.) *Die Musik in Geschichte und Gegenwart. Allgemeine Enzyklopädie der Musik* 9: 2318-2380. Kassel, Basel, Paris, London, New York, Prag: Bärenreiter/Stuttgart, Weimar: Melzler.

During, J. and A. Dick 2001a. Setar, in S. Sadie (ed.) *New Grove Dictionary of Music and Musicians* 23: 168-169. London: MacMillan Press Limited.

During, J. 2001b. Azerbaijan, in S. Sadie (ed.) *New Grove Dictionary of Music and Musicians* 2: 268-272. London: MacMillan Press Limited.

During, J. and J. Baily 2001c. Dutâr, in S. Sadie (ed.) *New Grove Dictionary of Music and Musicians* 7: 767-769. London: MacMillan Press Limited.

During, J. 2001d. Hand Made. Pour une anthropologie du geste musical. *Cahiers d'ethnomusicologie* 14: 39-68.

During, J. 2012. The dotâr family in Central Asia. Organological and musicological survey. *Porte Akademik. Organoloji sayasi*: 93-102. Istanbul.

Eberhard W. 2011. *Minstrel Tales from Southeastern Turkey: Folklore Studies V5.* Whitefish (Montana): Literary Licensing, LLC.

Egner, M. 1950. *Die Musikinstrumente des Alten Orients.* Münster: Aschendorffsche Verlagsbuchandlung.

Eichmann, R. 1987/1988. Zwei Schalen-Spiesslauten aus einer Spätzeitlichen Nekropole bei Abusir El-Meleq. *Jahrbuch der Berliner Museen* 29/30: 7-36.

Eichmann, R. 1988. Zur Konstruktion und Spielhaltung des altorientalische Spießlauten von den Anfängen bis in die seleukidisch-parthische Zeit. *Baghdader Mitteilungen* 19: 583-625.

Eichmann, R., P. Päffgen and N. Beyer 2000. Lauten, in L. Finscher (ed.) *Die Musik in Geschichte und Gegenwart. Allgemeine Enzyklopädie der Musik* 5: 942-994. Kassel, Basel, Paris, London, New York, Prag: Bärenreiter/Stuttgart, Weimar: Melzler.

Eichmann, R. 2004a. The Design of Ancient Egyptian Spike Lutes. E. Hickmann and R. Eichmann (eds). *Studien zur Musikarchäologie IV*: 363-371.

Eichmann, R. 2004b. Neuaufnahme einer Schalen-Spießlaute von Deir-el-Medina (Grab 1389)/ Ägypten. Hickmann E. and R. Eichmann (eds). *Studien zur Musikarchäologie IV*: 551–568.

Eldarova, E. 1964. Saz – Osnovnoij muzykal'nye instrument azerbajdzanskich ašugov. *Izvestya akademii nauk azerbajdžanskoj SSR. Serija obščestvennych nauk* 2: 109-119.

Elschek, O. 1967. Typologische Arbeitsverfahren bei Volksmusikinstrumenten. *Studia instrumentorum musicae popularis* I: 23-40.

Engel, C. 1870. *Descriptive Catalogue of the Musical Instruments in the South Kensington Museum.* London: Science and Art Department of the Committee of the Council on Education, South Kensington Museum.

Erdener, Y. 1995. *The Song Contest of Turkish Minstrels: Improvised Poetry Sung to Traditional Music.* New York and London: Garland Publishing.

Erdener Y. 1997. The Initiatory Dream of Turkish Minstrels. *International Journal of Music in Turkey. Journal of the Turkish Society for Musicology* 1, 3-4: 3-14.

Erdener, Y. 2001. Turkish Song Duel, in V. Danielson, S. Marcus and D. Reynolds (eds) *The Garland Encyclopedia of World Music. The Middle East* Volume 6: 801-809. London and New York: Routledge.

Erdener, Y. 2017. *Kars'ta Çobanoğlu Kahvehanesi'nde Âşık Karşılaşmaları. Âşıklık Geleneğinin Şamanizm ve Sufizmle Olan Taihsel Bağları.* Istanbul: Yapı Kredi Yayınları.

Erdmann, K. 1959. Serailbauten des 13. und 14. Jahrhunderts in Anatolien. *Ars Orientalis* 3: 77-94.

d'Erlanger, R. 2008. *La musique arabe* (6 vols.) Paris: Paul Geuthner, 1930-1959.

Eroğlu, S.C. 2017. Die Stellung der *kopuz* in der türkischen Volksmusik, in Çiftçi, N. and M. Greve (eds) *Die Bağlama in der Türkei und Europa. Erstes Bağlama-Symposium in Deutschland. Berlin, 14-15 September 2013*: 165

Ersoy, Ö. 2015. *Leerboek voor Bağlama, Bağlama Method.* Berlin: Ries und Erler.

Ertuğ, A. 1991. *The Seljuks. A Journey Through Anatolian Architecture.* Istanbul: Ahmet Ertuğ.

Erzincan, E. 1998. *Parmak vurma tekniğinin bağlamada uygulanışı ve notasyonu.* Bitirme Çalışması. Istanbul: Türk Musikisi Devlet Konservatuarı Temel Bilimler Bölümü.

Erzincan, E. 2019. *Bağlama İçin Besteler. Compositions for Bağlama. Bağlama, Bozuk, Misket ve Müstezat Düzenlerinde. In Bağlama, Bozuk, Misket and Müstezat Tunings.* Istanbul: Temkeş.

Farmer, H.G. 1925. Byzantine Musical Instruments in the Ninth Century. *Journal of the Royal Asiatic Society* 57: 299-304.

Farmer, H.G. 1926. The Evolution of the Tanbūr or Pandore. *Transactions of the Glasgow University Oriental Society* 26-27: 26-28.

Farmer, H.G. 1930. The Origin of the Arabian Lute and Rebec. *Journal of the Royal Asiatic Society* 62: 767-783.

Farmer, H.G. 1937. *Turkish Instruments of the Seventeenth Century as Described in the Siyâhat nâma of Ewliyâ Chelebî.* Translation edited with notes. Glasgow: The Civic Press.

Farmer, H.G. 1939. The Structure of the Arabian and Persian Lute in the Middle Ages. *Journal of the Royal Asiatic Society* 71: 41-51.

Farmer, H.G. 1962. Abdalqādir Ibn Ûaibí on Instruments of Music. *Oriens* 15: 242-248.

Farmer, H.G. 1964. Iranian Musical Instruments in the Ninth/Fifteenth Century. *Islamic Culture.* Volume 38 (3): 175-182.

Farmer, H.G. 1965. *The Sources of Arabian Music.* Leiden: E.J. Brill Academic Publishers.

Farmer, H.G. 1989. *Islam.* Musikgeschichte in Bildern. Musik des Mittelalters und der Renaissance. Band III, Lieferung 2. Begründet von H. Besseler und M. Schneider. Herausgegeben von W. Bachmann. Leipzig: VEB Deutscher Verlag für Musik.

Farmer, H.G. and J-C. Chabrier 2000. Tunbûr. *Encyclopaedia of Islam* X: 624-628.

Feldman, W. 1996. *Music of the Ottoman Court. Makam, Composition and the Early Ottoman Instrumental Repertoire.* Intercultural Music Studies. Volume 10. Berlin: VWB – Verlag für Wissenschaft und Bildung.

Fonton, C. 1751. *Essai sur la musique orientale comparée à la musique européene.* Paris.

Forry, M. 2000 Serbia, in T. Rice, J. Porter and C. Goertzen (eds) *The Garland Encyclopedia of World Music. Europe* Volume 8: 940-956. London and New York: Routledge.

Forry, M. 2000. Croatia, in T. Rice, J. Porter and C. Goertzen (eds) *The Garland Encyclopedia of World Music. Europe* Volume 8. London and New York: Routledge.

Franke, D. 2000 *Museum des Institutes für Geschichte der Arabisch-Islamischen Wissenschaften. Beschreibung der Exponate. Teil 1: Musikinstrumente.* Beschrieben von Daniël Franke unter Mitwirkung von Eckhard Neubauer. Frankfurt: Museum des Institutes für Geschichte der Arabisch-Islamischen Wissenschaften.

Galpin, F.W. 2011. *The Music of the Sumerians and their Immediate Successors, the Babylonians and Assyrians.* Cambridge: Cambridge University Press.

Garthwaite, G.R. 2005. *The Persians.* Oxford: Blackwell Publishing.

Gazimihâl, M.R. 1941. Halk şiirlerindeki musiki izleri. *Halk Bilgisi Haberleri* 10: 73-77.

Gazimihâl, M.R. 1960. Saz. *Türk Folklor Araştırmaları* 6: 2299-2300.

Gazimihâl, M.R. 1961. *Musiki Sözlüğü.* Istanbul: Mili Eğitim Bakanlığı.

Gazimihâl, M.R. 1975. *Ülkelerde Kopuz ve Tezeneli Sazlarımız.* Kültür Bakanlığı Milî Folklor Araştırma Dairesi Yayınları: 15. Ankara: Ankara Üniversitesi Basımevi.

Gazimihâl, M.R. 1991. Türk Halk Oyunları Katalog (3 Cilt). Ankara: Ankara Üniversitesi Basımevi.

Gojkovič, A. 1989. *Narodni muzički instrumenti* [Folk Instruments]. Belgrade.

Gojkovič, A. 1990. *Proučavanje narodnih muzičkih instrumenata u* Srbiji [The study of Musical Instruments in Serbia]. Belgrade.

Gojkovič, A. 1994. *Muzički instrumenti: mitovi I legende, symbolika I funkcija* [Musical Instruments: myths, legends, symbolism and function]. Belgrade.

Greve, M. 2003. *Die Musik der imaginären Türkei. Musik und Musikleben im Kontext der Migration aus der Türkei in Deutschland.* M&P Schriftenreihe für Wissenschaft und Forschung. Stuttgart, Weimar: Metzler-Verlag.

Greve, M. 2018. *Makamsiz: Individualization of Traditional Music on the Eve of Kemalist Turkey* (Istanbuler Texte und Studien, Band 39). Würzburg, Ergon Verlag.

Gsir, S. and E. Mescoli 2015. *Maintaining national culture abroad - Countries of origin, culture and diaspora*. INTERACT RR 2015/10, Robert Schuman Centre for Advanced Studies, San Domenico di Fiesole (FI): European University Institute.

Günaydın, K. 2004. *Karkamış in the First Millenium B.C.: Sculpture and Propaganda*. Master Thesis. Department of Archeology and History of Art. Bilkent University Ankara.

Haidar, M. 2002. *Central Asia in the Sixteenth Century*. New Delhi: Manohar Publishers and Distributors.

Hamadeh, S. 2007. *The City's Pleasures: Istanbul in the Eighteenth Century*. Washington (DC): University of Washington Press.

Hammarlund, A., T. Olsson and E. Özdalga (eds) 2001. *Sufism, Music and Society in Turkey and the Middle East*. Transactions Volume 10. Istanbul: Swedish Research Institute in Istanbul.

Harper, P.O. 1965. The Heavenly Twins. *The Metropolitan Museum of Art Bulletin, January*: 186-195. New York: The Metropolitan Museum of Art.

Harper, P.O. and P. Meyers 1981. *Silver Vessels of the Sasanian Period. Volume One: Royal Imagery*. New York: The Metropolitan Museum of Art.

Hassan, S.Q. 1982. The Long Necked Lute in Iraq. *Asian Music. Journal of the Society for Asian Music* 13 (2): 1-18.

Hassan, S.Q., R. Conway Morris, J. Baily and J. During 2001a. Tanbūr, in S. Sadie (ed.) *New Grove Dictionary of Music and Musicians* 25: 61-62. London: MacMillan Press Limited.

Hassan, S.Q. 2001b. Musical Instruments in the Arab World, in V. Danielson, S. Marcus and D. Reynolds (eds) *The Garland Encyclopedia of World Music. The Middle East* Volume 6: 407-408. London and New York: Routledge.

Hassan, S.Q. 2001c. Syria, in S. Sadie (ed.) *New Grove Dictionary of Music and Musicians* 24: 852-857. London: MacMillan Press Limited.

Hemetek, U. *Mosaik der Klänge - Musik der ethnischen und relgiösen Minderheiten in Österreich*. Wien: Böhlau Verlag.

Henke, B. 2002. *Untersuchungen zur altmesopotamischen Laute und ihrer sozio-kulturellen Stellung*. Wissenschaflichen Hausarbeit zur Erlangung des akademischen Grades einer Magistra Artium der Universität Hamburg. Hamburg: Universität Hamburg. Fachbereich Orientalistik. Studiengang Altorientalistik.

Henrotte, G.A. 1992. Music and Gesture: A semiotic Enquiry. *The American Journal of Semiotics* 9 (4): 103-114.

Hickmann, H. 1961. *Ägypten*. Musikgeschichte in Bildern. Musik des Altertums. Band II, Lieferung 1. Begründet von H. Besseler und M. Schneider. Herausgegeben von W. Bachmann. Leipzig: VEB Deutscher Verlag für Musik.

Higgins, R.A. and R.D. Winnington-Ingram 1965. Lute-players in Greek art. *The Journal of Hellenic Studies* 85: 62-71.

Hızır Ağa (Kemânî) 1793. *Tefhîmü'l-Makamat fi Tevlîdi'n-Nağamât*. Istanbul: Topkapı Sarayı Kütüphanesi.

Hodgson, M.G.S. 1963. The Interrelations of Societies in History. *Comparative Studies in Society and History* 5: 227-250.

Hodgson, M.G.S. 1993. *Rethinking World History. Essays on Europe, Islam, and World History*. Cambridge: Cambridge University Press.

Hoerburger, F. 1975. Langhalslauten in Afghanistan. *Asian Music. Journal of the Society for Asian Music* 6: 28-37.

Holst, G. 1994. *Road to Rembetika. Music of a Greek sub-culture, Songs of Love, Sorrow and Hashish*. Limni, Evia, Greece: Denise Harvey.

Hopkin, B. 1996. *Musical Instrument Design: Practical Information for Instrument Making*. Tucson (Arizona): Sharp Press.

Hornbostel, E.M. von and C. Sachs 1914. Systematik der Musikinstrumente. Ein Versuch. *Zeitschrift für Ethnologie* 46: 553-590.

Ilerici, K. 1948. *Türk musikîsi tonal sistemi ve armonisi*. Istanbul.

Inalcık, H. 1973 *The Ottoman Empire. The Classical Age 1300-1600*. London: Phoenix.

Inalcık, H. 2003. *Şaîr ve Patron*. Ankara. Doğu Batı Yayınları.

Irwin, R. 2006. *The Lust of Knowing. The Orientalists and their Enemies*. London: Allen Lane.

Issawi, C. 1989. Empire Builders, Culture Makers, and Culture Imprinters. *Journal of Interdisciplinary History* 20: 177-196.

Jäger, R.M. and U. Reinhard 2000. Türkei, in L. Finscher (ed.) *Die Musik in Geschichte und Gegenwart. Allgemeine Enzyklopädie der Musik* 9: 1049-1079. Kassel, Basel, Paris, London, New York, Prag: Bärenreiter/Stuttgart, Weimar: Melzler.

Jeliazkov, K., R. Sirakov and L. Vladimirov 2005. *Tanbur Bulghary. Book for the Bulgarian Tamboura*. Kibea.

Jenkins, J.L. and P.R. Olsun 1976. *Music and Instrumental Instruments in the World of Islam*. London: World of Islam Festival Publishing Company.

Kachulev, I. 1978. *Bulgarian Folk Musical Instruments*. Pittsburgh.

Kahraman-Yücel Dağlı, A. 2005. *Günümüz :Türkçesiyle Evliya Çelebi Seyahatnâmesi Istanbul*. Istanbul: Yapı Kredi Yayınları.

Karababa, H. 2005. *Bağlamanin tarihçesi*. Ankara: Anadolu Medeniyetleri Kültür Merkezi Yayınıdır.

Karomatov, F.M., V.A. Meškeris and T.S. Vyzgo 1987. *Mittelasien*. Musik des Altertums. Band II, Lieferung 9. Begründet von H. Besseler und M. Schneider. Herausgegeben von W. Bachmann. Leipzig: VEB Deutscher Verlag für Musik.

Kellner-Heinkele, B. and D. Rohwedder (eds) 1985. *Turkische Kunst un Kultur aus osmanischer Zeit*. Recklinghausen: Verlag Aurel Bongers.

Kennedy, H. (ed.) 2002. *A Historical Atlas of Islam*. Leiden: E.J. Brill Academic Publishers.

Kerimov, M. 2003. *Azarbaycan musiqi alatlari. The Azarbaijan musical instruments*. Baku: Yeni Nasıl Publishing House.

Kılıç, F. (ed.) 2010. *Aşık Çelebi Meşâ'ir üş-Şu'arâ. Inceleme-metin*. Istanbul: Araştırma Enstitüsü.

Kircher, A. 1650. *Musurgia universalis sive ars magna consoni et dissoni*. Rome.

Kirsch, D. 2001. Colascione, in S. Sadie (ed.) *New Grove Dictionary of Music and Musicians* 6: 92-93. London: MacMillan Press Limited.

Kiwan, N. and U.H. Meinhof 2011. Music and Migration: A Transnational Approach. *Music and Arts in Action* 3, Issue 3.

Köksel, B. 2012. *Kadın Âsıklar. 20. Yüzyıl Âşık Geleneğinde*. Ankara: Akçağ Yayınları.

Kolar, W.W 1973. *A History of the Tambura*. Vol. 1. Pittsburgh, Pennsylvania: Duquesne University Tamburitzans. Institute of Folk Arts.

Kolar, W.W. 1975. *A History of the Tambura 2: The Tambura in America*. Pittsburgh, Pennsylvania: Duquesne University Tamburitzans. Institute of Folk Arts.

Kononenko Moyle, N. 1990. *The Turkish Minstrel Tale Tradition*. New York and London: Garland Publishers.

Koperdraat, M. 2004. Tríchordo versus tetráchordo. *Lychnari*, 2004/3.

Koperdraat, M. 2017. De baglamás, roemrucht en geliefd. *Lychnari*, 2017/1.

Köprülü, M.F. (ed.) 1940. *Türk sâz şairleri II: Antoloji, XVI-XVIII asırlar*. Istanbul.

Köprülü, M.F. 1964. *Türk Saz-şairleri (19. Yüzyıl Saz Şairleri)*. Ankara: Milti Kültür Yayınları.

Köprülü, M.F. 2011. Early Mystics in Turkish Literature. London and New York: Routledge.

Kremenkev, B.A. 1952. *Bulgarian-Macedonian Folk Music*. Oakland (California): University of California Press.

Kuronen, D. 2004. Beauty for Eye and Ear, in *MFA Highlights Musical Instruments*. Museum of Fine Arts. Boston: 11-19.

Kurt, I. 1989. *Bağlamada düzen ve pozisyon*. Istanbul: Pan Yayıncılık.

Kurt, N. 2016. Alevi-Bektaşi Cemlerinde "Deste Bağlama" Geleneği ve "Bağlama" Adının Kaynağı. *EÜ Devlet Türk Musikisi Konservatuvarı Dergisi* 8: 43-62.

Laborde, J.B. de 1780. *Essai sur la musique ancienne et moderne*. A Paris, De l'Imprimérie de PH. - D. Pierres, Imprimeur ordinaire du Roi; Et se vend chez Eugène Onfroy, Libraire, rue du Hierepoix. M.DCC.LXXX. Avec Approbation, et du Roi. Tome Premier. Livre Premier. Livre II. Des Instruments Chapitre XVIII. Des Instruments Arabes: 379-385. Paris.

Landels, J.G. 1999. *Music in Ancient Greece & Rome*. London and New York: Routledge.

Lawergren, B., H. Farhat and S. Blum 2001. Iran, in S. Sadie (ed.) *New Grove Dictionary of Music and Musicians* 12: 521-546. London: MacMillan Press Limited.

Leotsakos, G. and J.C. Sugarman 2001. Albania, in S. Sadie (ed.) *New Grove Dictionary of Music and Musicians* 1: 282-289. London: MacMillan Press Limited.

Levin, T. 2001a. Central Asia: Overview, in V. Danielson, S. Marcus and D. Reynolds (eds) *The Garland Encyclopedia of World Music. The Middle East* Volume 6: 895-906. London and New York: Routledge.

Linin, A. 1970. Šarkija kod albanaca na Kosovu [The Šarkija among the Albanians of Kosova]. *Glasnik Muzeja Kosova/Buletini Muzeut të Kosovës*: 355-370.

Lundberg, L. 2002. *Historical Lute Construction*. Tacoma (WA): Guild of American Luthiers.

Mahillon, V-C. 1893-1922. *Catalogue descriptif & analytique du Musée instrumental du Conservatoroire royla de musique de Bruxelles*. Bruxelles: T. Lombaerts.

Manukian, M. 2001. Music of Armenia, in V. Danielson, S. Marcus and D. Reynolds (eds). *The Garland Encyclopedia of World Music. The Middle East* Volume 6: 723-738. London and New York: Routledge.

Manniche, L. 1975. *Ancient Egyptian Musical Instruments*. Müncher Ägyptologische Studien. München: Deutscher Kunstverlag.

Marâghî (Abd al-Qadir Ibnu Ghaibî al-Marâghî) 1977. *Maqâsid al-Alhân*. Teheran: Taqi Bîniš. Zendigi.

Marâghî (Abd al-Qadir Ibnu Ghaibî al-Marâghî) 1987. *Jâmi' al-Alhân*. Teheran: Taqi Bîniš. Mash'al.

March, R. 2013. *The Tamburitza tradition. From the Balkans to the American Midwest*. Madision: University of Wisconsin Press.

Marcuse, S. 1975. *Musical Instruments. A Comprehensive Dictionary*. New York: W.W. Norton & Company.

Markoff, I. 1990/1991. The Ideology of Musical Practice and the Professional Turkish Folk Musician: Tempering the Creative Impulse. *Asian Music. Journal of the Society for Asian Music* 22-1: 129-145.

Markoff, I. 2001a. Aspects of Turkish Folk Music Theory, in V. Danielson, S. Marcus and D. Reynolds (eds). *The Garland Encyclopedia of World Music. The Middle East* Volume 6: 59-76. London and New York: Routledge.

Markoff, I. 2001b. Alevi Identity and Expressive Culture, in V. Danielson, S. Marcus and D. Reynolds (eds). *The Garland Encyclopedia of World Music. The Middle East* Volume 6: 793-800. London and New York: Routledge.

Martin, R. Sarây-ı Enderûn. Albert Bobowski (Ali Ufki) from the French manuscript of 1666. *Turkish Music Quarterly* 3/4: 1-3.

Masterpieces of Persian Painting. 2011. Tehran Museum of Contemporary Art. Tehran.

Mathiesen, T.J. 1999. *Apollo's Lyre. Greek Music and Music Theory in Antiquity and the Middle Ages.* Lincoln (NE): University of Nebraska Press.

Mathiesen, T.J., D. Conomos, G. Leotsakos, S. Chianis and R.M. Brandl 2001. Greece, in S. Sadie (ed.) *New Grove Dictionary of Music and Musicians* 10: 327-359. London: MacMillan Press Limited.

Manteghi, H. *Alexander the Great in the Persian Tradition. History, Myth and Legend in Medieval Iran.* I.B. London: Tauris, 2018.

Matzner J. 1970. *Zur Systematik der Borduninstrumente.* Strasbourg, Baden-Baden: Editions PH Heitz. Verlag Heitz.

McCarthy, J. 1997. *The Ottoman Turks. An Introduction History to 1923.* London and New York: Longman.

McKinnon, J.W. 2001. Pandoura, in S. Sadie (ed.) *New Grove Dictionary of Music and Musicians* 19: 30.

Montagu, J. 1980. *The World of Medieval & Renaissance Musical Instruments.* Woodstock (New York). The Overlook Press.

Montagu, J. 2006. The Creation of New Instruments. *The Galpin Society Journal* LIX: 3-11.

Montagu, J. 2007. *Origins and Development of Musical Instruments.* Lanham (Maryland): Scarecrow Press.

Montagu, J. 2009. 'It's time to look at Hornbostel-Sachs again'. *Muzyka* i: 7-27.

Moore, J.K., J. Dobney and E.B. Strauchen-Scherer (eds) 2015. *Musical Instruments: Highlights of the Metropolitan Museum of Art.* New York: The Metropolitan Museum of Art.

Nagy, G. 1995. *The Song Contest of Turkish Minstrels. Improvised Poetry Sung to Traditional Music.* New York and London: Garland Publishers.

Navagero, B. 1553. 'Relazione dell'Impero Ottomano del Clarissimo Bernardo Navagero, Stato Bailo a Costantinopoli Fatta in Pregadi nel Mese di Febbrajo del 1553,' in *Relazioni degli Ambasciatori Veneti al Senato*, ed. Eugenio Albèri, III, v.1. Florence: Tipografia e Calcografia all'Insegna di Clio, 1840: 72–73.

Neubauer, E. 1965. *Musik am Hof der Frühen 'Abassiden.* Frankfurt: Museum des Institutes für Geschichte der Arabisch-Islamischen Wissenschaften.

Neubauer, E. 1969. Musik zur Mongolenzeit in Iran und den angrenzenden Ländern. *Der Islam* 45: 233-260.

Neubauer, E. 1993. Der Bau der Laute und ihre Besaitung nach arabischen, persischen und türkischen Quellen des 9. Bis 15. Jahrhunderts. *Zeitschrift für Geschichte der Arabisch-Islamischen Wissenschaften* III: 279-377.

Neubauer, E. (ed.) 1999. Der Essai sur la musique orientale von Charles Fonton mit Zeichnungen von Adanson. *The science of music in Islam*, 4. Frankfurt: Museum des Institutes für Geschichte der Arabisch-Islamischen Wissenschaften.

Neubauer, E. and V. Doubleday 2001. Islamic Religious Music, in S. Sadie (ed.) *New Grove Dictionary of Music and Musicians* 12: 599-610. London: MacMillan Press.

Niebuhr, C. 1992. *Reisenbeschreibung nach Arabien und andern umliegenden Ländern.* Zürich: Manesse Verlag.

Olssun, T., E. Özdalga and C. Raudva (eds) 1998. *Alevi Identity. Cultural, Religious and Social Perspectives.* Volume 8. Istanbul: Swedish Research Institute in Istanbul.

Omerzel-Terlep, M. Slovenia, in T. Rice, J. Porter and C. Goertzen (eds) *The Garland Encyclopedia of World Music. Europe* Volume 8. London and New York: Routledge.

Overy, R (ed.) 2004. *Complete History of the World*. New York: Times Books.

Özbek, M. 1998. *Türk halk müziği el kitabı I. Terimler sözlüğü*. Ankara: Atatürk Kültür Merkezi Başkanlığı Yayınları.

Özcan, N. 1998. *Türk Mûsikîsinde Tanbur Sazının Gelişimi*. Doktora Tezi. Istanbul: Marmara Üniversitesi, Sosyal Bilimler Enstitüsü, Islâm Tarihi Ve Sanatları Anabilim Dali Türk Din Mûsikîsi Bilim Dali.

Özergin, M.K. 1971. Instruments in the Ottoman Empire in the 17th century. *Turkish Folklore Researches*. I (no 262), II (no 263), III (no 264), IV (no 265).

Özgür, E. 2013. *Lehrbuch für Bağlama. Bağlama Method*. Berlin: Ries & Erler.

Öztürk, O.M. 2016. Geleneksel Bağlama Icrasının Gelisiminde Üstadlik Kültürünün Rolü ve Belirleyiciliği (The Role and Determinance of the Culture of Mastership in the Development of Traditional Bağlama Performance, in A. Koç *1st Uluslararasi Nida Tüfekçi Bağlama Sempozyumu. Istanbul Teknik Üniversitesi ITÜ). Türk Devlet Konservatuari*: 125-142.

Pahlevanian, A., A. Kerovpyan and S. Sarkisyan 2001. Armenia, in S. Sadie (ed.) *New Grove Dictionary of Music and Musicians* 2: 10-28. London: MacMillan Press Limited.

Papuga, D.W. 1995. *The Folk, the State and the Prophets. Poetry, Music and Politics in a Turkish Province*. PhD dissertation, Department and Museum of Antropology, University of Oslo.

Parlak, E. 2000. *Türkiye›de el ile (şelpe) bağlama çalma geleneği ve çalış teknikleri*. Ankara: TC Kültür Bakanlığı.

Parlak, E. 2001. *El İle Bağlama Çalma (Şelpe) Tekniği Metodu 1*. Istanbul: Ekin Yayınları.

Parlak, E. 2005. *El İle Bağlama Çalma (Şelpe) Tekniği Metodu 2*. Istanbul: Alfa-Aktüel Yayınları.

Parlak, E. 2011. *Erol Parlak Bağlama (Saz) Okulu - Schule - Method. Parmak Tekniği (Şelpe) İçin Sistematik Kılavuz, Cilt 1/Eine systematische Anleitung für die Fingerspieltechnik (Şelpe) Technique*, Vol. 1. Willemshaven: Acoustic Music Books.

Parlak, E. 2013. *Garip Bülbül Neşet Ertaş. Hayatı - Sanatı - Eserleri* (2 cilt). Istanbul: Demos Yayınları.

Peacock, A.C.S. and S.N. Yildiz 2012. *The Seljuks of Anatolia: Court and Society in the Medieval Middle East*. London: I.B. Tauris.

Peacock, A.C.S. and D.G. Tor (eds) 2015. *The Medieval Central Asia and the Persiante World: Iranian Tradition and Islamic Civilization*. London: I.B. Tauris.

Pekin, E. 2003. Sûrnâme'nin müziği: 16. yüzyılda Istanbul'da çalgılar. *Dop Not* 1: 52-90. Istanbul: Minar Sinan Üniversitesi Güzel Sanatlar Fakültesi.

Pekin, E. 2004. Theory, Instruments and Music, in H. Inalcık and G. Renda (eds). *Ottoman Civilization 2*: 1008-1043. Ankara: Republic of Turkey, Ministry of Culture and Tourism.

Pekin, E. 2014. Evliya Çelebi'nin çalgı listleri. *Istanbul Araştırmaları Yıllığı* 3: 51-77.

Pekin, E. 2018. Surname'nin müziği 2: 18. yüzyıl başlarında Istanbul'da müzik, in A. Erdoğdu, Z. Atbaş and A. Çötelioğlu (eds) *Filiz Cağman Armağan*: 455-528. Istanbul: Lale Yayıncılık.

Pekin, E. 2019. Şeştar: Anadolu'nun çalgısı, in N.S. Turan and S.E. Çak (eds). *Şehvar Beşiroğluya Amarğan*: 129-161. Istanbul: Pan Yayıncılık.

Petropoulos, E. 2000. *Songs of the Greek Underworld*. The Rebetika Tradition. London: Saqi Books.

Petrov, S., M. Manolova and D.A. Buchanan 2001. Bulgaria, in S. Sadie (ed.) *New Grove Dictionary of Music and Musicians* 4: 569-583. London: MacMillan Press Limited.

Petrović, A. 2000. Bosnia-Hercegovina, in T. Rice, J. Porter and C. Goertzen (eds) *The Garland Encyclopedia of World Music. Europe* Volume 8. London and New York: Routledge.

Picken, L. 1975. *Folk Musical Instruments of Turkey*. Oxford: Oxford University Press.

Pirker, M. 1993. K. Atatürks reform und das Musikleben in der Türkei. *Musicologica Austriaca* 12: 33-39.

Poché, C. 2001b. Musical Life in Aleppo and Syria, in V. Danielson, S. Marcus and D. Reynolds (eds) *The Garland Encyclopedia of World Music. The Middle East* Volume 6: 565-571 London and New York: Routledge.

Poulton, D. 1987-1988. The Early History of the Lute. *Journal of the Lute Society of America* 20-21: 1-22.

Pourtahmasi, K. and A.S. Golpayegani 2009. *Introducing Mulberry's wood (Morus alba L) used in bowl shaped musical instruments of Iran.* Actes de la journée d'étude *Le bois: instrument du patrimoine musical.* Paris: Cité de la Musique.

Prudhomme, D. 2014. *Rebetiko.* Istanbul: Aylak Kitab.

Racy, A.J. 2001. Lebanon, in S. Sadie (ed.) *New Grove Dictionary of Music and Musicians* 14: 419-429. London: MacMillan Press Limited.

Rashid, S.A. 1984. *Mesopotamien.* Musikgeschichte in Bildern. Musik des Altertums. Band II, Lieferung 2. Begründet von H. Besseler und M. Schneider. Herausgegeben von W. Bachmann. Leipzig: VEB Deutscher Verlag für Musik.

Rault, T. 2000. *Musical Instruments. A Worldwide Survey of Music-Making.* London: Thames and Hudson.

Recueil de cent estampes représentant différentes nations du Levant, gravées sur les tableaux peints d'apres nature en 1707 & 1708 par les ordres de M. de Ferriol. M. Le Hay, Paris, 1714.

Reichl, K. 2007. Turkic oral epic poetry from Central Asia, in E. Çağatay and D. Kuban (eds). *The Turkic speaking peoples. 2,000 Years of art and culture from Inner Asia to the Balkans*: 54-68. München: Prestel and Prins Claus Fund Library.

Reinhard, K. 1981. Turkish Miniatures as Sources of Music History. Music East and West: Esays in honour of Walter Kaufmann. *Festschrift Series* 3: 143-166.

Reinhard, K and U. Reinhard 1984. *Musik der Türkei. Band 1: Die Kunstmusik. Band 2: Die Volksmusik.* Internationales Institut für vergleichende Musikstudien. Wilhelmshaven: Heinrichshofen's Verlag.

Reinhard, K., M. Stokes and U. Reinhard 2001. Turkey, in S. Sadie (ed.) *New Grove Dictionary of Music and Musicians* 25: 909-921. London: MacMillan Press Limited.

Reinhard, U. and T. de Oliveira Pinto 1989. *Sänger und Poeten mit der Laute. Türkische Âşık und Ozan.* Staatlichen Museen Preußischer Kulturbesitz, Berlin. Veröffentlichungen des Museums für Völkerkunde Berlin. Neue Folge 47. Abteilung Musikethnologie VI. Berlin: Dietrich Reimer Verlag.

Revision of the Hornbostel-Sachs Classification of Musical Instruments by the MIMO Consortium 2011. *MIMO H-S classification.*

Rice, T., J. Porter and C. Goertzen (eds) 2000a. *The Garland Encyclopedia of World Music. Europe* Volume 8. London and New York: Routledge.

Rice, T. 2000b. Bulgaria, in T. Rice, J. Porter and C. Goertzen (eds) *The Garland Encyclopedia of World Music. Europe* Volume 8: 890-910. London and New York: Routledge.

Rice, T. 2004. *Music in Bulgaria. Experiencing Music, Expressing Culture.* Oxford: Oxford University Press.

Robinson, F. 1998. *The Cambridge Illustrated History of the Islamic World.* Cambridge: Cambridge University Press.

Roxburgh, D.J. (ed.) 2005. *Turks a Journey of a Thousand Years 600-1600 AD.* London: Royal Academy of Arts.

Rushton, J. 2001. Quarter-tone, in S. Sadie (ed.) *New Grove Dictionary of Music and Musicians* 20: 661-662. London: MacMillan Press Limited.

Russel, A. and P. Russel 1794. *The Natural History of Aleppo*. London: G.G. and J. Robinson.

Ruthven, M. 2004. *Historical Atlas of the Islamic World*. Oxford: Oxford University Press.

Sachs, C. 1913. *Real-Lexicon der Musikinstrumente. Zugleich ein Polyglossar für das gesamte Instrumentengebiet*. Berlin: Julias Bard Verlag.

Sachs, C. and E.M. von Hornbostel 1914. Systematik der Musikinstrumente. Ein Versuch. *Zeitschrift für Ethnologie* 46 (4-5): 553-590.

Sachs, C. 1929. *Geist und werden der Musikinstrumenten*. Berlin: Dietrich Reimer Verlag.

Sachs, C. 1930. *Handbuch der Musikinstrumentenkunde. Band XII. Kleine Handbücher der Musikgeschichte nach Gattungen*. Hrsgb von H. Kretzschman. Leipzig: Breitkopf & Härtel, 1930.

Sachs, C. 1940. *The History of Musical Instruments*. New York: W.W. Norton.

Sachs, C. 1943. *The Rise of Music in the Ancient World, East and West*. New York: W.W. Norton.

Sağ, A. and E. Erzincan 2009. *Bağlama Metodu. Bağlama Method. Bağlama Düzeni. Bağlama Tuning. Cilt I ve II. Alıştırmalar ve Repertuvar. Exercise and Repertoire*. Volume I and II. Istanbul: Pan Kitab.

Said, E. 1978. *Orientalism*. New York: Pantheon.

Şare, T. 2017. Women and Music in Ancient Anatolia. The Iconographic evidence, in E. Kozal, M. Akar, Y. Heffron, Ç. Çilingirolu, T.E. Şerifoğlu, C. Çakrlar, S. Ünlüsoy and E. Jean (eds). *Questions, Approaches, and Dialogues in Eastern Mediterranean Archaeology. Studies in Honor of Marie-Henriette and Charles Gates*: 555-580. Münster: Ugarit-Verlag.

Sarı, A. 2012. *Türk Müziği Çalgıları. Ud, Tanbur, Kanun, Kemençe, Ney, Kudum*. Istanbul: Nota Yayıncılık.

Sárosi, B. 1967. *Handbuch der europäischen Volksmusikinstrumente. Die Volksmusikinstrumente Ungarns. Serie I - Band 1*. Leipzig: VEB Deutscher Verlag für Musik.

Sarısözen, M. 1940. *Çok sesli müzik ve bağlamalar. Güzel Sanatlar, sayı 2*. Ankara.

Savory, R. 1980. *Iran under the Safavids*. Cambridge: Cambridge University Press.

Sawa, G.D. 1989. *Music Performance Practice in the Early cAbbâsid Era 132-320 AH / 750-932 AD*. Ontario: Pontifical Institute of Mediaeval Studies.

Sawa, G. 2001. Classification of Musical Instruments in the Medieval Middle East, in V. Danielson, S. Marcus and D. Reynolds (eds) *The Garland Encyclopedia of World Music. The Middle East* Volume 6: 881-892. London and New York: Routledge.

Saz, L. 1994. *The Imperial Harem of the Sultans: Daily Life at the Çirağan Palace during the 19th Century: Memoirs of Leyla (Saz) Hanimefendi*. Istanbul: Peva Publications.

Schimmel, A. 1975. *Mystical Dimensions of Islam*. Chapel Hill: The University of North Carolina Press.

Schippers, H. 2010. *Facing the Musik, Shaping Music Education from a Global Perspective*. Oxford: Oxford University Press.

Schossig, D. 2010. *Der Colascione - eine Langhalslaute des 17./18. Jh*. Großmehring.

Schuol, M. 2000. Darstellungen von hethitischen Musikinstrumenten unter Berücksichtigung der Schriftzeugnisse. *Orient-Archäologie* 7: 159-170.

Schuol, M. and S. Kammerer 1998. Vorderasien, in L. Finscher (ed.) *Die Musik in Geschichte und Gegenwart. Allgemeine Enzyklopädie der Musik* 9: 1766-1816. Kassel, Basel, Paris, London, New York, Prag: Bärenreiter/Stuttgart, Weimar: Melzler.

Sefercioğlu, M.N. 1999. Dîvan Şiirinde Mûsikî Ile Ilgili Unsurların Kullanılışı'. *Osmanlı* 9: 649-668.

Shields, Sarah (2013). The Greek-Turkish Population Exchange: Internationally Administered Ethnic Cleansing. *Middle East Report* (267): 2-6.

Shiloah A. 1995. *Music in the World of Islam. A Socio-Cultural Study.* Detroit: Wayne State University Press.

Shiloah, A. 2000. Arabische Musik, in L. Finscher (ed.) *Die Musik in Geschichte und Gegenwart. Allgemeine Enzyklopädie der Musik* 1: 686-766. Kassel, Basel, Paris, London, New York, Prag: Bärenreiter/Stuttgart, Weimar: Melzler.

Shirazi, N. 2002. *Setar Construction. An Iranian Musical Instrument.* Teheran: PART Publications.

Siminoff, R.H. 2008. *Siminoff's Luthiers Glossary.* Milwaukee (Wisconsin): Hall Leonard Books.

Sims, E. 2002. *Peerless Images. Persian Painting and its Sources.* New Haven and London: Yale University Press.

Sint Nicolaas, E., D. Bull, and G. Renda 2003. De Ambassadeur, de Sultan en de Kunstenaar. Op audiëntie in Istanbul. Rijksmuseum Dossiers. Amsterdam: Rijksmuseum Amsterdam.

Sirojiddinov, S. 2018. *Mir 'Alî Shîr Navâ'î the Great.* Tashkent.

Slobin, M. and R. Sultanova 2001. Dömbra, in S. Sadie (ed.) *New Grove Dictionary of Music and Musicians* 7: 439-440. London: MacMillan Press Limited.

Slobin, M., A. Djumaev and L. Dodhoudoyeva 2001. Tajikistan, in S. Sadie (ed.) *New Grove Dictionary of Music and Musicians* 25: 14-19. London: MacMillan Press Limited.

Smentek, K. 2010. Looking East. Jean-Étienne Liotard, the Turkish Painter. *Ars Orientalis* 39: 85-111.

Smith, D.A. 2002. *A History of the Lute from Antiquity to the Renaissance.* Lute Society America.

Sokoli, R. and P. Miso 1991. *Veglat muzikore të popullit shqiptar* (Musical Instruments of the Albanian People). Tirana.

Soucek, S. 2000. *A History of Inner Asia.* Cambridge: Cambridge University Press.

Sodøy, R.I. and M. Leman (eds) 2010. *Musical Gestures. Sound, Movement, and Meaning.* London: Routledge.

Soydas, E. 2007. Osmanlı Sarayında Çalgılar (Instruments of the Ottoman Court). PhD dissertation, Istanbul Technical University.

Spector, J., R. At'Ajan, C. Rithman C and R. Conway Morris 2001. Saz, in S. Sadie (ed.) *New Grove Dictionary of Music and Musicians* 22: 361-362. London: MacMillan Press Limited.

Stauder, W. 1973. *Alte Musikinstrumente in ihrer vieltausendjährigen Entwicklung und Geschichte.* Braunschweig: Klinkhardt und Biermann.

Steblin, R. 1995. The Gender Stereotyping of Musical Instruments in the Western Tradition. *Canadian University Music Review / Revue de musique des universités Canadian* 16 (1): 128-144.

Stockmann, E. 1971. The Diffusion of Musical Instruments in an Inter-Ethnic Process of Communication. *Yearbook of the Internation Folk Music Council*: 128-141.

Stokes, M.H. 1993. *The Arabesk Debate. Music and Musicians in Modern Turkey.* Oxford: Claredon Press.

Stokes, M.H. 1999. Turkey. Sounds of Anatolia, in S. Broughton, M. Ellingham and R. Trillo (eds). *World Music, Africa, Europe and the Middle East* 1: 396-410. London: Rough Guides.

Stokes, M.H. 1999. The media and reform: the saz and elektrosaz in urban Turkish Folk Music. *British Journal of Ethnomusicology* 1: 89-102.

Sugarman, J. 2000. Albanian Music, in T. Rice, J. Porter and C. Goertzen (eds) *The Garland Encyclopedia of World Music. Europe* Volume 8: 986-1007. London and New York: Routledge.

Sultanova, R. 2011. *From Shamanism to Sufism: Women, Islam and Culture in Central Asia.* London: I.B. Tauris.

Sultanlar, Tüccarlar, Ressamlar. 2012. *Türk-Hollanda İlişkilerinin Başlangıcı. Sultans, Merchants, Painters. Turkish-Dutch Relations*. Istanbul: Suna ve Inan Kıraç Vakfı, Pera Müzesi.

Sümer F., A.E. Uysal and W.S. Walker (eds) 1991. *The book of Dede Korkut*. Austin: University of Texas Press. Austin.

Szendrai, J., D. Legány, J. Kapáti, M. Berlász, P. Halász, B. Sárosi and I. Kertész Wilkinson 2001. Hungary, in S. Sadie (ed.) *New Grove Dictionary of Music and Musicians* 11: 846-871. London: MacMillan Press Limited.

Talam, J. 2013. Folk Musical Instruments in Bosnia and Herzegovina. Cambridge: Cambridge Scholars Publishing.

Tekelioğlu, O. 2001. Modernizing Reforms and Turkish Music in the 1930s. *Turkish Studies* 2: 93-108.

Tekin, O. (ed.) 2019. *Hellenistik ve Roma Dönemlerinde. Krallar, İmparatorlar, Kent Devletleri. Hellenistic and Roman Anatolia. Kings, Emperors, City States*. Istanbul: Yapı Kredi Yayınları.

Thompson, J. and S.R. Canby (eds) 2004. *Hunt for Paradise. Court Arts of Safavid Iran 1501-1576*. New York: Skira.

Titley, N.M. 1983. *Persian Miniature Painting*. Austin: University of Texas Press.

Todorov, M. 1973. *Bulgarski narodi muzikalni instrumenti: organografiya* [Bulgarian Folk Musical Instruments: an Organology]. Sofia.

Tolgahan, Ç. 2011. *The Adaptation of Bağlama Techniques into Classical Guitar Permance*. Saarbrücken: VDM Verlag Dr. Müller.

Tozlu, M. 2014. Âsım Divânı'nda Mûsikî Unsurlar. *Divan Edebiyatı Araştırmaları Dergisi* 13: 141-166.

Tromans, N., C. Riding, A.J. Marciari and E. Hughes (eds) 2008. *Doğun Cazibesi. Britanya Oryantalist Resmi. The Lure of the East. British Orientalist Painting*. Istanbul: Suna ve Inan Kiraç Vakfı, Pera Müzesi.

Tucker, J. 2003. *The Silk Road. Art and History*. London: Philip Wilson Publisher.

Turan, M., G. Öz and O. Yılmaz 1999. *Dostlar Seni Unutmadı/The Friends Still Rember You*. Ankara, Türkiye Cumhuriyeti Kültür Bakanlığı.

Turnbull, H. 1972. The Origin of the Long-necked Lute. *The Galpin Society Journal* 25: 58-66.

Turnbull, H. 2006. The Genesis of Carvel-Built Lutes. *Musica Asiatica* 1: 75-84.

Turner, C. 2006. *Islam. The Basics*. London: Routledge.

Tursun Bey (ed. Tulum, M.) 1977. *Târîh-i Ebü'l-Feth*. Istanbul: Baha Matbaası.

Uslu, R. 2015. *Selcuklu Topraklarında* Müzik. Konya: Konya Valiliği Il Kültür ve Turizm Müdürlüğü.

Uzunçarşılı, I.H. 1977. Musical Life at the Palaces in the Ottoman Era. *Belleten* XLI/161: 79-114.

Vertkov, K.N., G.I. Blagodatov and E.E. Jazovickaya 1975. *Atlas muzykal'nych instrumentov naradov SSSR (Atlas of the Musical Instruments of the Peoples inhabiting the USSR)*. Moscow: Muzyka.

Villoteau, G-A. 1823. *Description de l'Égypte ou recueil des observations et de recherches qui ont été faites en Egypte pendant l'expédition de l'armée française, publié par les orders de sa majesté l'empereur Napoléon le Grand*. État moderne. Tome premier. *Description historique, technique et littéraire des instruments de musique des orientaux*. Première Partie. *Des instrumens a cordes connus en Egypte*. Second Édition. Dédiee au Roi. Paris: Publiée par C.L.F. Panckoucke.

Villoteau, G-A. 1823. Planches. Planche AA, Tome 2. In *Description de l'Égypte ou recueil des observations et de recherches qui ont été faites en Egypte pendant l'expédition de l'armée française, publié par order du gouvernement de sa majesté l'empereur Napoléon le Grand*. Second Édition. Dédiee au Roi. Tome treizième. État moderne. Paris: Publiée par C.L.F. Panckoucke.

Vukosavljev, S. 1990. *Vojvodjanska tambura* [The Tanbur in Vojvodina]. Novi Sad.

Wachsmann, K., J.W. McKinnon, R. Anderson, J. Harwood, D. Poulton, D. Van Edwards, L. Sayce and T. Crawford 2001. Lute, in S. Sadie (ed.) *New Grove Dictionary of Music and Musicians* 15: 329-363. London: MacMillan Press Limited.

Warland, R. 2013. Byzantinisches Kappadokien. Darmstadt Mainz: Verlag Philipp von Zabern.

Weber, S. and U. al-Khamis 2014. *The Artistic Legacy of Umayyad Damascus and Abbasid Baghdad (650-950). Early Capitals of Islamic Culture.* München: Hirmer Verlag.

Wegner, M. 1963. Griechenland. Musikgeschichte in Bildern. Musik des Altertums. Band II, Lieferung 4. Begründet von H. Besseler und M. Schneider. Herausgegeben von W. Bachmann. Leipzig: VEB Deutscher Verlag für Musik.

Wegner, U. 1989. 'Ûd, in L. Finscher (ed.) *Die Musik in Geschichte und Gegenwart. Allgemeine Enzyklopädie der Musik* 9: 1089-1102. Kassel, Basel, Paris, London, New York, Prag: Bärenreiter/ Stuttgart, Weimar: Melzler.

Werner, K. and B.R. DeWalt (eds) 2012. *MIM Highlights from the Musical Instrument Museum.* Phoenix: The Musical Instrument Museum (MIM).

West, M.L. 1992. *Ancient Greek Music.* Oxford: Claredon Press.

Worrel, W.H. 1948. Notes on the Arabic Names of Certain Musical Instruments. *Journal of the American Oriental Society* 68 (1): 66-68.

Yastıman, Ş. 1959. *Sazdan düzenler.* Istanbul.

Yekta, R. 1922. La musique Turque. *Lavignac Encyclopédie de la Musique et Dictionnaire du Conservatoire.* Tome 5: 2945-3064. Paris: Librairie Delagrave.

Yenisey, F. 1946. *Bektaşî Kadın Neşriyat Şairlerimiz, Pazar Neşriyat Yurdu.* Izmir.

Yılmaz, G. 2015. Bektaşilik ve Istanbul'daki Bektaşi Tekkeleri Üzerine Bir İnceleme. *Osmanlı Araştırmaları. The Journal of Ottoman Studies* XLV: 97-136.

Youssefzadeh, A. 2002. *Les bardes du Khorassan iranien. Le bakhshi et son répertoire.* Travaux et mémoires de l'Institut d'études iraniennes. Leuven – Paris: Diffusion Peeters.

Zeeuw, J. de 2009. *De Turkse langhalsluit of bağlama.* Amsterdam.

Zeeuw, J. de 2018. The Ottoman tanbûr. Introducing the Long-Necked Lute of Ottoman Classical Music. *Expedition* 60 (2): 24-37.

Zeeuw, J. de 2019. *Tanbûr Long-Necked Lutes along the Silk Road and beyond.* Oxford, Archaeopress.

Illustration Credits

The author and publisher thank the following sources for their kind permission to reproduce illustrations in this book. Every effort has been made to contact copyright holders for permission to reproduce illustrations in this book. The publisher would be grateful to hear from any copyright holder who is not acknowledged here and will undertake to rectify any errors or omissions in future editions of this book.

Figure 1.	© Jean-Benjamin de Laborde. *Essai sur la musique ancienne et moderne.*
Figure 2.	© Villoteau, G-A. *Description de l'Égypte ou recueil des observations et de recherches qui ont été faites en Egypte. Des instrumens a cordes connus en Egypte.*
Figure 3.	© Trustees British Museum, London.
Figure 4.	© Courtesy Ricardo Eichmann, Berlin.
Figure 5.	© Author, Ankara Archeological Museum, Ankara.
	© Yapı Kredi Yayınları, Istanbul.
Figure 6.	© Author, British Museum, London.
	© Courtesy National Archaeological Museum, Athens.
Figure 7.	© Iraq Museum, Baghdâd.
	© Staatlichen Museen, Vorderasiatisches Museum, Berlin.
Figure 8.	© Courtesy Freer Gallery of Art, Smithsonian Institution, Washington.
Figure 9.	© Museum für Islamische Kunst, Staatliche Museen, Berlin.
Figure 10.	© Yeni Nasıl Publishing House, Baku.
Figure 11.	© Hellenic Institute of Byzantine and Post-Byzantine Studies, Venice.
Figure 12.	© Chester Beatty Library, Dublin.
	© Yeni Nasıl Publishing House, Baku.
Figure 13.	© EKAV /Eğitim Kültür ve Araştırma Vakfı, Istanbul.
Figure 14.	© Topkapı Sarayı Müzesi, Istanbul.
	© Topkapı Sarayı Müzesi, Istanbul.
Figure 15.	© Topkapı Sarayı Müzesi, Istanbul.
	© Topkapı Sarayı Müzesi, Istanbul.
Figure 16.	© Staatlichen Museen Kunstbibliothek, Berlin.
	© Bibliothèque National de France, Paris.
Figure 17.	© Topkapı Sarayı Müzesi, Istanbul.
Figure 18.	© Le Département des Estampes de la Photographie, Paris.
Figure 19.	© Kemânî Hızır Ağa. *Tefhîmü'l Makamat fi Tevlîd-in Neğamât.*
	© Istanbul Üniversitesi Kütüphanesi, Istanbul.
Figure 20.	© Christie's auction of Old Master Paintings, 2004.
Figure 21.	© Ignace Mouradjea d'Ohsson. *Tableau Général de l'Empire Othoman, divisé en deux parties, dont l'une comprend la Législation Mahométane; l'autre l'Histoire de l'Empire Othomane.*
Figure 22.	© M. de Ferriol. *Recueil de cent estampes représentant différentes nations du Levant, gravées sur les tableaux peints d'apres nature en 1707 & 1708 par les ordres de M. de Ferriol.*
Figure 23.	© The Walters Art Museum, Baltimore.
Figure 24.	© Author, Musée du Louvre, Paris.

Figure 25.   © Musée du Quai Branly, Paris.
Figure 26.   © Museum of Turkish and Islamic Art, Istanbul.
                © Yapı Kredi Yayınları, Istanbul.
Figure 27.   © Yapı Kredi Yayınları, Istanbul.
Figure 28.   © Courtesy Ergun Çağatay, Istanbul.
Figure 29.   © Marie-Gabriel-Florent-Auguste Comte de Choiseul-Gouffier. *Voyage
                pittoresque de la Grèce*.
                © Courtesy Atlas of Plucked Instruments, the Netherlands.
Figure 30.   © Villoteau, G-A. *Description de l'Égypte ou recueil des observations et de recherches
                qui ont été faites en Égypte. Des instrumens a cordes connus en Égypte*.
                © Alexander Russell. *The Natural History of Aleppo*.
Figure 31.   © Copyrights unknown.
                © Courtesy Karl Kirchmeyr, Vienna.
Figure 32.   © Courtesy Denise Harvey (Publisher), Greece.
                © Courtesy Melissa Publishing House, Athens.
Figure 33.   © Âşık Veysel Ailesi Fotoğraf Arşivi.
Figure 34.   © Cafer Açın / Author, Istanbul.
Figure 35.   © Cafer Açın / Author, Istanbul.
Figure 36.   © Author.
Figure 37.   © Courtesy Yavuz Gül, Izmir.
                © Courtesy Denise Harvey (Publisher), Greece.
Figure 38.   © Courtesy Engin Topuzkanamış, Izmir.
Figure 39.   © Kulsan Foundation, Amsterdam.
Figure 40.   © Courtesy Efrén López, Spain.
Figure 41.   © Courtesy Kemal Dinç, Germany.
Figure 42.   © Courtesy Cafer Açın, Istanbul.
Figure 43.   © Author.
Figure 44.   © Courtesy Jérôme Cler, France.
Figure 45.   © Author.
Figure 46.   © Unknown source.
Figure 47.   © Author.
Figure 48.   © Author/Engin Topuzkanamış, Istanbul, Izmir.
Figure 49.   © Author/Engin Topuzkanamış, Istanbul, Izmir.
Figure 50.   © Courtesy Cafer Açın, Istanbul.
Figure 51.   © Courtesy Engin Topuzkanamış, Izmir.
Figure 52.   © Author.
Figure 53.   © Courtesy Engin Topuzkanamış, Izmir.
Figure 54.   © Author.
Figure 55.   © Courtesy Engin Topuzkanamış, Izmir.
Figure 56.   © Courtesy Cafer Açın, Istanbul.
Figure 57.   © Courtesy Oxford University Press, Oxford.
Figure 58.   © Courtesy Kulsan Foundation, Amsterdam, Topkapı Sarayı Müzesi, Istanbul.
                © Cafer Açın, Istanbul.
Figure 59.   © Author.
Figure 60.   © Author.
Figure 61.   © Cafer Açın / Author, Istanbul.
Figure 62.   © Courtesy Dietrich Reimer Verlag, Berlin.

Figure 63.   © Author.
                  © Unknown source.
Figure 64.   © Unknown source.
Figure 65.   © Author.
Figure 66.   © Courtesy Ulaş Özdemir, Istanbul.
Figure 67.   © Author.
Figure 68.   © Author.
Figure 69.   © Author.
Figure 70.   © Author.

A Note on Turkish

Turkish belongs to the Altaic language group that originates in the border region of Mongolia and Kazakhstan. The Turkish alphabet broadly corresponds to the English alphabet. There are a number of letters that the English alphabet does not have: ç, ğ, ı, ö, ş, ü and a number that is pronounced differently: c, g, j, u, v, y. The letters ij, q, w and x are not part of the Turkish alphabet. The letter w does appear in a number of borrowings. With some loan words from Arabic and Persian there are long pronounced vowels. An ā or â is pronounced as a long aa, ī or î as ee and ū or û as oo, which is emphasized. Here ^ ('circumflex') is chosen. For Turkish words and proper names the modern Turkish spelling has almost always been used.

The pronunciation of the Turkish letters is as follows:

c	as *j* in *jam*
ç	as *ch* in *chat*
g	as in get
ğ	is almost silent tending to lengthen the preceding vowel, e.g. *bağlama*
j	zj
ö	eu
ş	sj
u	oe
ü	uu
v	w
y	j

Index